W9-CCB-539

MONTREAL

in your pocket

MICHELIN

Travel Publications

MAIN CONTRIBUTOR: PAUL GLASSMAN

PHOTOGRAPH CREDITS
Photos supplied by The Travel Library:
Winston Fraser front cover, 3, 23(t), 35, 47, 63, 87,
111; Michael Klinec back cover, title page, 5, 8, 9,
11, 13, 16, 18, 21, 22, 23(b), 26, 27, 28, 30(t,b), 31,
32, 33, 34, 36, 39, 40, 41, 42, 43, 44, 45, 46, 48, 49,
50, 51, 53, 55, 56, 59, 61, 64, 66, 68, 73, 74, 75,
78(t,b), 79, 80, 81, 82, 83, 84, 92, 93, 98, 100, 103,
107, 116, 119, 125; Tourisme Montreal 113.
Other Photos:
Tourisme Québec 25, 76, 88(t,b), 89, 90, 105.

Front cover: The Illuminated Crowd *sculpture in front
of the Tour BNP ;*
back cover: the St Lawrence, with Old Montreal beyond;
title page: Plateau Mont-Royal district.

MANUFACTURE FRANÇAISE DES PNEUMATIQUES MICHELIN

Place des Carmes-Déchaux – 63000 Clermont-Ferrand (France)

© Michelin et Cie. Propriétaires-Éditeurs 2001

Dépôt légal Jan 01 – ISBN 2-06-000196-X – ISSN 1272-1689

No part of this publication may be reproduced in any form

without the prior permission of the publisher.

Printed in Spain 01/01

MICHELIN TRAVEL PUBLICATIONS
Hannay House
39 Clarendon Road
WATFORD Herts WD17 1JA - UK
☎ (01923) 205240
www.ViaMichelin.com

MICHELIN TRAVEL PUBLICATIONS
Michelin North America
One Parkway South
GREENVILLE, SC 29615
☎ 1-800 423-0485
www.ViaMichelin.com

CONTENTS

INTRODUCTION

Ah, Montreal. Ahhh, Montréal.

Whether you pronounce it '*mon-tree-all*' or '*mon-ray-ahl*', the city brings a smile to the face of anyone who's visited, lived there, or longed to touch down. Other cities have statistics to support their notoriety – taller buildings or important banks, or key industrial achievements. Montreal is a manufacturing center, a railroad hub, one of the great ports on the continent, and, increasingly, a high-tech center. But Montreal also has *savoir faire*, its own way of doing things.

Montreal skyline at night, viewed from Mount Royal.

Take a quick look from an airplane, or as you approach by car, and you'll see a city of skyscrapers, monumental Olympic Park architecture, a network of expressways, and expansive suburbs reaching far into the hinterlands – and right in the middle, a green mountain. Zoom in a little closer. Montreal is clean, cheery and safe – people stroll Rue Sainte-Catherine at all hours, even in winter. Walk a few blocks from the busy modern downtown, and you'll find yourself in Old Montreal, the virtually intact 19C city. Around *carrés* and parks, venerable churches lend an Old World atmosphere and recall the outpost of European civilization in the wilderness. The city is packed with surprises below its slick surface – literally. If the weather's too hot, too cold or too wet for your liking, plunge into the neighborhoods of the Underground City. Head north a few blocks from the city center, and you're a world away, in the woods of Mount Royal Park.

Immerse yourself in the French-language environment – only Paris has more French-speakers. Beyond the French influence is the Latin character that makes Montreal such a treat to explore. Montrealers have fun and flair, and weave enjoyment into work, business and every aspect of life. And the visitor too can enjoy the wonderful juxtaposition of the best of so many worlds: North American efficiency ... earthy *québécoise* hospitality and superb service ... fast food with a Continental touch and fine cuisine ... throbbing nightlife, riverside parks and endless spaces ... French spoken everywhere, but English widely understood, and sometimes Cantonese and Greek as well.

It all clashes yet blends together, inviting you to take part – and usually at a surprisingly affordable price. This is the excitement of Montreal.

GEOGRAPHY

Montreal lies on an island 50km long by 17km wide (31 by 10 miles), where the Ottawa River meets the St Lawrence, the major waterway from the Atlantic to the heart of the continent.

Mount Royal, topped by its signature cross, is emblematic of the city, a gentle rise that forms a backdrop to the skyscrapers of downtown. It's part of a mountain chain that steps across the bed of an ancient sea. A gaze from the mountain's lookouts reveals inner neighborhoods stretching away to suburbs of individual houses. An archipelago of smaller islands, mostly green, dots the St Lawrence and its fertile valley. Ocean-going ships sail the deep waters, a journey of a thousand kilometers from the Gulf of St Lawrence, into Montreal's port. The Laurentian Mountains rise only 40km (25 miles) to the north. To the south and east are the more distant peaks of the Appalachians; to the west, a series of lakes formed by wide river bends and confluences.

Montreal is a northern city, subject to extremes. Winters are long, but not endlessly bitter. Winds and weather systems can move from the south and west, as well as the polar regions. Summer days are generally refreshing – there are muggy exceptions, to be sure – and with long northern daylight, they go on, and on.

HISTORY

The exceptional geography of Montreal island – its setting and its connection to the world – has largely determined its history. For its aboriginal inhabitants, the Mohawks of the **Iroquois** nation, rising ground afforded protection from spring floods. The river made for ease of trade, while the heights of the mountain provided a lookout for the approach of rival Iroquois clans. Essentially farmer-hunters, the Iroquois lived in wooden long-houses, following a simple life growing crops, hunting and fishing – until this was destroyed by the arrival of Europeans.

A French Outpost

Jacques Cartier was the first Frenchman to explore the St Lawrence River, in search of gold and a north-west passage to Asia. Landing on an island in the river in 1535, he came across a Huron Indian village, **Hochelaga**, on the site of today's city. He is said to have climbed Mount Royal, which he christened Mont Réal, after his king.

Due note was taken of the presence of 'heathen souls', but they were to remain undisturbed for a further 75 years or so, until **Samuel de Champlain** made further explorations in 1603, and established a fur-trading post at Place Royale in 1611. French interest in the area lay not only in its strategic importance but also

The Montreal skyline in autumn.

Traditional Mohawk long-house, at Kahnawake.

A way of life was transplanted from the motherland, took hold, and developed after its own fashion. Governors sent from France held overall authority and supervised defense. Orders of priests and nuns looked after not only spiritual matters, but education and health, and were economic powers. Sister Jeanne Mance founded the Hôtel-Dieu, a hospital order, in 1644. Sister Marguerite Bourgeoys established the first school in 1658.

French law was adapted to local conditions. The first land concessions were granted in 1648. *Seigneurs*, holders of estates, upheld public order and tradition in the feudal system, and controlled the livelihoods of their tenant farmers. Mining and fur concessions brought income to the crown. By 1660, large amounts of pelts were moving through the settlement, which had become the center of trading in North America. Yet the Indian nations were not always under control. The settlers of Lachine, just upriver, were massacred in 1689. Eventually a settlement with the Iroquois was reached in 1701, with the signing of a **peace treaty**, though hostilities still arose from time to time.

Montreal grew, but slowly. By 1681 its inhabitants numbered 1 418. If not exactly as prosperous as the West Indies at the time, New France was strategic, control-

in the wealth it could derive from the abundant resources here – notably fur. France's intentions moved beyond mere commerce in 1642 when the mission settlement of Ville-Marie de Montréal, numbering some 50 Frenchmen, was founded by **Paul de Chomedey, Sieur de Maisonneuve**. Its purpose was to convert the Indians to Christianity, and, not incidentally, to reinforce French control.

The path to conversion was not a smooth one, and Ville-Marie was precariously held at first. Missionaries sent farther inland were occasionally massacred. Difficulty in raising crops under unfamiliar conditions, uncertain provisioning from France, and seemingly endless winters all took their toll. But Ville-Marie and the settlements downriver held on, and grew. Well inland, they were safe from the British navy.

ling rivers to the interior of the continent. As other European powers contended to control the Americas, conflict over the territory was inevitable, notably with the British with whom the French were already doing battle in Europe.

The British took coastal Acadia (Nova Scotia) in 1713, and expelled its French colonists in 1755. England kept a wary eye on the French settlements on the St Lawrence when hostilities resumed in 1756. The clifftop fortress downriver at Quebec seemed impregnable – until a night-time landing gave the enemy entry to the Plains of Abraham. What transpired in a ferocious battle just minutes long, in 1759, is called the **Victory of the Plains of Abraham** by English Canadians – and is still known as *la conquête* (the conquest) or *la défaite* (the defeat) by French-speakers in Canada. The

commanding officers on both sides were killed, French regular troops were overwhelmed, and the fate of the continent was changed. In the wake of the disaster, Montreal for a time became the capital of the colony, but it too surrendered to the British in 1760.

British Control

New France passed to the English crown. Yet Montreal did not quite become an English town. Under the **Quebec Act** of 1774, the British Parliament granted religious tolerance to its Catholic subjects in Canada, and French civil law and the seigniorial system were maintained. French Canadian civil society continued to flourish, guided by the religious orders, if not by France. Priests encouraged their flocks to cultivate the land, or to enter the priesthood, the law, or one of the few approved professions. When

Remains of the city's original French fortifications, Champ de Mars.

public education was eventually established, it was with separate systems for Catholics (largely French) and Protestants.

Allegiance to the French crown quickly passed to the English. When American Revolutionary invaders occupied Montreal in 1775, they expected to find anti-English sentiment and willing allies. **Benjamin Franklin** was part of a delegation that attempted to win over the population to the Revolutionary cause. To no avail. The Americans withdrew to fight elsewhere. Another invasion, in 1812, likewise found no local support, and was rebuffed.

In the wake of the American Revolution, Tories fled northward. An English-speaking society developed, parallel to but separate from the French one, based on commerce and the consolidation of Britain's grasp on its remaining North American dominions. The largely French-speaking colony of Lower Canada (Quebec) was separated from the increasingly English Upper Canada (Ontario) in 1791.

Metropolis of Canada

Montreal grew, reaching a population of 20 000 in 1800; by 1801, it became necessary to demolish the great stone walls surrounding what is now Vieux-Montréal that limited the expansion of the city. At first, the **fur trade** and river transport were the basis of Montreal's expansion. The North-West Company, founded by Simon McTavish in 1784, engaged in a bitter rivalry with the Hudson's Bay Company for control of the fur trade. The two rivals merged in 1821, diverting fur exports away from Montreal to Hudson Bay, and Montreal's importance was briefly reduced.

However, lumber, wood products and mining picked up the slack, and the city's position as a transportation hub was reinforced when the Lachine Canal opened in 1825, allowing smaller vessels to bypass rapids on the St Lawrence to reach the Great Lakes. Goods were transferred from ocean-going ships to canal vessels in the port of Montreal. Industry followed, including textile manufacture, taking advantage of water power and easier access to supplies. Later, railroads reached out to cross the continent from the inland port. The first tracks reached Lachine in 1847. The Victoria Bridge brought rail traffic from the south in 1859. By 1886, trains ran across the continent to Vancouver.

The settlement of the Canadian west, the transportation of grain from newly established farms, the provisioning of the settlements with British manufactures, all meant growth for Montreal. The capital was mostly British, the entrepreneurs were

Scottish or American, and the backs on which the city was built were often Irish, especially after the potato famine in Ireland. Fortunes were created in short order, and the nouveau captains of industry – William Van Horne of the Canadian Pacific Railroad, and others – built their mansions in the Golden Square Mile along Sherbrooke Street, then a peripheral area at the base of Mount Royal.

Center of Power

With commerce came political power, and also political conflict. The great influx of immigrants from Scotland, England and Ireland not only fuelled the economic boom, but also meant that for the first half of the 19C Montreal was a largely English-speaking city. French-speakers felt disadvantaged in the new economy of the day, and marginalized in politics, as well. The French sat in the legislature, but the English kept political control through an appointed governor and council. Rebellion by French Canadians anxious for a greater say in politics broke out in 1837, and riots raged in Montreal. In 1844 Montreal, now with a population of 44 000, became capital of United Canada, a status that was to last only until 1849, when rioters set fire to the parliament building on Place d'Youville. The

Canadian, Quebec and Montreal flags flying outside Marché Bonsecours, once the seat of government of United Canada.

Constitution Act of 1867, ratified by the British Parliament, combined the four provinces of Quebec, Ontario, New Brunswick and Nova Scotia to form the **Canadian Confederation** – a new political entity designed to give the Canadians more political power.

Changing City

As ties with Britain loosened over the years, Montreal became less of a colonial center, and more a world-class metropolis. The 20C saw continued industrialization, the extension of streetcar lines, and the erection of some of the major office buildings in Canada.

Montreal became more cosmopolitan. Blacks migrated from the States to work on the expanding railroads and to live under a less oppressive social regime. The Chinese who had built the railways came to settle, followed by immigrants from eastern and southern Europe.

Yet Montreal also returned to its Quebec roots. The city expanded from its original walled enclosure, up the escarpment, onto the slopes of Mount Royal, and outward, absorbing neighboring towns, all of them French-speaking. With migration from the countryside and a higher birth rate among Catholics, Montreal became a majority French-speaking city once again. Long-existing fissures between French and English deepened. Opposition to conscription was widespread among French Canadians in both World Wars. Where once English- and French-speakers had alternated as mayor, under a gentleman's agreement, French Canadians took firm control of the political reins, with the support and the cooperation of the still largely English-speaking business class.

During the post-World War II period known as **La Révolution Tranquille** (The Quiet Revolution), Church authority began to break down – a precursor of changes in Catholic Ireland, Spain and Italy. Stereotypical huge families, aspirations to the priesthood, and orphanages full of unwanted babies were things of the past. French and English Montrealers began to live and act more like each other, and French-speakers began to exert their presence in all fields.

The French Canadian nationalist movement, always a powerful cultural force, became reinvigorated politically. Beyond long-standing demands for autonomy in cultural and linguistic matters, the French wanted what the English had: management positions, money, and, ultimately, secular power. Through work and political change, they made inroads. The provincial government nationalized power generation in

The St Lawrence Seaway.

Montreal and the rest of Quebec, then directed public investment toward *Québecois* enterprises.

At its Peak

By the mid 20C, Montreal became a leader in urban design in cold climates, with the construction of vast complexes such as Place Ville-Marie, where shopping arcades were sheltered from the extremes outside.

Under **Mayor Jean Drapeau**, the city went on a spending spree to make it a modern and monumental city. The metro, an ultra-modern subway system running on rubber tires, was constructed. Expressways were forged around, through, and even under the center of the city, and new bridges spanned the St Lawrence River. The St Lawrence Seaway opened in 1959, for the first time allowing ocean-going vessels to reach the Great Lakes. Montreal's vibrancy was celebrated with a world fair – **Expo 67** – and with the **Olympic Games** in 1976.

Second Place

Underneath the shining, cosmopolitan surface, however, there were cracks. The Olympics saddled Montreal with a debt that, some 24 years later, has not been repaid. After the Seaway opened, Montreal continued as an important depot and cargo-transfer point. Yet many ships passed it by. Industry began a slow but inevitable shift westward. Rival Toronto became more than an upstart, eventually surpassing Montreal in size and economic activity.

The tensions between Canada's two main linguistic groups were played out in the city where they most often encountered each other. French Canadian nationalists sought more cultural and economic control within Quebec, either within Canada, or through outright *séparation* – secession.

A small minority was willing to use violence to achieve its goals. In 1970 the Front de Libération du Québec kidnapped a British trade official and murdered a provincial cabinet minister. Martial law was declared under the War Measures Act, at the request of the province. The crisis passed, but bitterness lingered over the presence of federal troops.

While the threat of violence waned, Quebec nationalism made inroads at the ballot box, and in 1976 the independence-minded **Parti Québécoise** stunned the establishment by taking power. Political instability was now added to the somewhat precarious situation of Montreal's economy. Major companies' head offices headed for Toronto, or farther west. With them went managers and English-speaking professionals. The absolute numbers were not great, but where once Montreal had attracted businesses, investment and entrepreneurs, the flow was now in the opposite direction.

French Power

Laws were changed, and with them, expectations. Immigrants were required to attend French-speaking schools, no matter what their origins. 'Languages other than French' – a euphemism for English – were excluded from business, public service, advertising and, as far as possible, from public view. The changes in the law applied throughout the province, but they only had an effect in Montreal. Montreal remained as cosmopolitan as ever, but the common language had changed.

Eventually, an equilibrium of sorts was reached on the language front. There are grumblings now and then, but people live and work together without fuss – as they had done for the most part in any case. Two referendums failed to produce secession from Canada, but that option is considered a legitimate one, even if on more or less indefinite hold.

Once the unemployment capital of Canada, Montreal has rushed back to prosperity. International organizations now move to Montreal to take advantage of multilingual workers, American-style amenities, a reasonable cost of living, recreation facilities, and a cosmopolitan ambience. Montreal remains as dynamic as it has ever been, while preserving its sense of history and continuation with its past. It's enough to attract many a visitor, too.

PEOPLE AND CULTURE

Language is People

How do you describe the people of Montreal – a million in the city limits, three million in the metropolitan area? On the surface, they appear to be overwhelmingly French-speaking. Quebeckers as a whole came from one small region of France, near St Malo, and have experienced remarkably little admixture. But take a look at the genealogy of Monsieur Aulèrie in Montreal and you'll find that his ancestor was Mr O'Leary from County Clare. Johnson and Ryan are typically French names here. On the other hand, there are Lapierres and Trudeaus who speak not a word of French, or who speak both languages but write only one, or who speak neither language particularly well.

In Montreal, language *is* ethnicity. A black athlete from the Dominican Republic who plays shortstop for the Montreal Expos baseball team is considered English (or *anglophone*, to use the local term). He communicates with his team mates, and the world at large, in that language.

Mr Goldstein, who grew up in Montreal and went to English-language schools, is English. Monsieur Lévy, whose parents came from Morocco in the 1950s, is French (*francophone*). They might or might not attend the same synagogue. On the other hand, Mr Papadopoulos and Señor Gómez speak Greek and Spanish at home respectively, so they're known by the peculiar Quebec term *allophone*. Chances are, their children switch effortlessly between three languages.

To complete the rich linguistic and cultural tapestry, there are Mohawk Amerindians from Kahnawake, just outside the city, who usually speak English, and Montagnais Amerindians named McKenzie from downriver who are most comfortable in French – though neither group would call itself English or French.

In rough terms, about two-thirds of the people on Montreal island (the City of Montreal and a couple of dozen suburbs) are French-speaking, though many speak English as well. Of the remainder, under half – 14 per cent – use English as their first language (only half of these are of British stock). The rest are *allophones*, native speakers of a third language, which in Quebec is usually, but not always, a stopping-point on the way to becoming *francophone*.

Ethnic Melting Pot

The story of Montreal, more so than the story of Quebec or Canada as a whole, is one of peoples dominating the territory and city in succession, or living in uneasy coexistence – Amerindians, French colonists, native-born *Canadiens*, British and later arrivals. Unquestioned French control lasted for little more than 100 years. After what French Canadians call 'the Conquest', in 1763, Montreal came to be dominated by immigrants from the British Isles. Irishmen provided the backs on which much of the expanding city was built, though, as Roman Catholics, many of them integrated with French-speaking society.

As in other Canadian cities, there is still a strong immigrant presence – about 20 per cent of the population is foreign-born, including, notably, Chinese and other Asians, and Latin Americans. Vibrant ethnic populations are the heritage of previous waves of immigration. The Jewish, Greek and Italian communities, now mostly native-born, are significant. Blacks came with the Underground Railroad, before the American Civil War, and later to serve on more solid railroads reaching across the country; today they make up about 5 per cent of the metropolitan population. Later arrivals, both English- and French-speaking, have come from the Caribbean.

The indigenous community, if not prominent in numbers – less than 1 per cent – is present. Montreal is a health and service center for remote Indian and Inuit communities to the north, while native communities such as Kahnawake thrive nearby, asserting their traditional rights and ways.

Two Cultures

Novelist Hugh McLennan used the term 'two solitudes' to describe the peaceful, if sometimes grudging, coexistence of the French and English for much of the last two centuries. English and French have lived side by side but their crossing-points have been less visible than their dividing line. Traditionally, this has been Boulevard St-Laurent, which of course has a different name in English: St Lawrence Boulevard or 'The Main'.

East of The Main were the working-class French districts, three-story apartment structures with trademark treacherous metal staircases on the outside. To the south-west were some of the Irish and Black districts, where the stairs were inside. The French

Aboriginal immigrants from Peru at the First Peoples' Festival.

elite, lawyers and doctors, resided in Outremont, in Second Empire houses. The English elite, captains of industry and business-men, first occupied the Golden Square Mile along Sherbrooke Street, then decamped westward to the heights of Westmount, a separate municipal enclave with its own Second Empire houses, Beaux Arts mansions and genteel row houses with porches.

McGill University occupies a priceless swathe of real estate on the edge of downtown, at the southern fringe of Mount Royal. The Université de Montréal occupies the northern fringe of the mountain, announcing its significance with its trademark tower by Ernest Cormier, one of the city's architectural gems.

In between, successive genera-tions of newer immigrants slipped in, generally occupying the dividing line. Levine's Bakery on The Main eventually became a Portuguese establishment. The St-Viateur Bagel Factory passed into Italian ownership.

The arts have flourished in the two main communities, but side by side, and hardly touching. Leonard Cohen, the songwriter, and Mordecai Richler, the novelist, are appreciated in English Montreal, in the rest of Canada, and elsewhere. But many a literate French-speaker has never touched their works. On the other hand, many an English

Montrealer has not heard of any novel by Gabrielle Roy, who chronicled the lives of the French working class, or seen a play by Michel Tremblay, portraying street and family life. Occasion-ally, there are crossovers. Ever hear of Céline Dion? And the home-grown Cirque du Soleil, breaking all moulds of what the big top should be, regularly sells out at two venues in Las Vegas.

Census figures tell us that the old divisions are breaking down. Intermarriage in Montreal between English- and French-speakers, once quite rare, is now common. English-speakers of the younger generation are usually fluent in French – and often get quite irritated with their elders, who either never learned the language or were not given the opportunity to do so in school.

While nationalists have largely succeeded in making French the common language, they've brought about an unexpected turn. English is still widely used and understood, if not always visible to the casual visitor. French-speakers want to learn more English in school. Young people want the best of both cultures. Linguistic conflict has led not to annihilation but (and not without sore points) to mutual appreciation. It's a Montreal solution. Everything finds its place, and it's all there to appreciate.

MUST SEE

Place d'Armes★
All Montreal, its tradition and its history, spreads before you from this square: **Notre Dame Basilica★★★** and traditional ecclesiastical power; **Vieux-Montréal★★★** (Old Montreal), where the city began; and the banks that stored the wealth of an expanding mercantile Canada.

Place Jacques-Cartier★★
At the heart of Old Montreal, sloping down toward the Old Port, this pedestrian area is always lively with buskers, peddlers and pavement cafés in a 19C setting.

Oratoire Saint-Joseph★★ (St Joseph's Oratory)
The faith that is at the heart of traditional French Canada is nowhere more emphatically and

movingly displayed than in this massive temple dedicated to miracles of healing.

Calèche Ride in Old Montreal★★★

Capture the grace of Montreal, its old-time ways cherished in the present, and the round of activities at the **Old Port★** at a gentle, clip-clop pace.

The Underground City★★★

Montrealers create comfort amid climatic extremes. There's no single attraction down under, but rather, the wonder of an ensemble of cheery and functioning underground neighborhoods.

Rue St-Denis at Night★

The heart of cosmopolitan Montreal beats loudest in the Latin Quarter, where bistros, fine restaurants, theaters, art movie houses and *café-terrasses* bring out strollers at all hours, in all seasons.

Parc du Mont-Royal★★
(Mount Royal Park)

The mountain is more than a green oasis of recreation. It's the emblem, the very name of the city, commanding **views★★** downtown, of the river and the countryside beyond from its heights.

Parc Olympique★★
(Olympic Park)

The **Olympic Park★★** represents the edifice complex at its height in Montreal. Love it or hate it, the leaning design of the **Olympic Tower** is undeniably daring, the **view★★★** from the top thrilling.

The exquisite interior of Notre Dame Basilica is breathtaking – its inspiring, graceful arches and the rich detail bathed in blue light.

How to See the City

Leave the car at home, or garage it after you arrive. For most of your stay, you can explore on foot. Montreal is compact, about 2km (1.2 miles) from Rue St-Denis west to Rue Guy, or from the St Lawrence River to the base of Mount Royal. Getting around is simple and quick. If it rains or snows, or turns hot and humid, simply plunge under the city. Montreal's extensive Underground City provides sheltered connections between places you'll want to see.

To explore further afield, Montreal has a clean, modern and efficient metro (underground) system, and buses (*see* p.126).

Orientation

The St Lawrence River, running north-eastward toward the Atlantic, is the main reference line in Montreal. Streets generally run parallel or at right angles to the river. As used by Montrealers, and in this book, 'east' and 'west' (*est* and *ouest* on street signs) mean 'downriver' and 'upriver' (though actually north-east and south-west).

All street signs are in French, but the corresponding English term is often used in conversation (St Catherine Street for Rue Sainte-Catherine). We will generally use the terms that you will see. North-south street numbers start at the St Lawrence River. Boulevard St-Laurent is the division between 'east' and 'west' numbers.

Opening Hours

Most **museums** are closed on Mondays, with exceptions noted. Opening times may be restricted outside the warmer months (especially for attractions at Parc Jean Drapeau, the islands opposite downtown). A bargain all-museum pass, usable over two days, is available at the Centre Infotouriste or at any museum.

VIEUX-MONTRÉAL★★★
(OLD MONTREAL)

A visit to Montreal logically starts where the city itself began. The waterfront district of Old Montreal was a backwater for many years, as the city grew and ascended the Montreal escarpment to today's downtown. Luckily, houses, churches, convents and mansions dating back to the colonial period were left intact, if neglected, by the city's re-focus. It was left to today's generation to restore these treasures. With gentrification and public investment, the old city has been reborn as a business and shopping neighborhood, entertainment center and upmarket residential

Old Montreal, which grew up next to the river, is remarkably well-preserved, while the modern city stretches away behind it.

area. When a horse-drawn carriage passes on a cobbled byway, you're back in the 19C.

Place d'Armes★

Start at the traditional heart of Montreal (*metro:* Place-d'Armes) (CY), the public square laid out over 300 years ago. All the markers of the city's development surround you. The **Maisonneuve monument★** (CY 1) honors Paul de Chomedey, Sieur de Maisonneuve, the founder of the city, who fought and defeated the Iroquois on this very spot.

To the south stands the imposing **Basilique Notre-Dame★★★** (Notre Dame Basilica), constructed between 1824 and 1829. The twin towers, 69m (226ft) high, named Temperance and Perseverance, are still striking landmarks although overshadowed by modern skyscrapers. The Gothic magnificence of the exterior continues inside with painted and sumptuous gilt woodwork, cascading into pulpits, and niches filled with saints, gleaming in natural and blue-tinted light. The eastern

The Maisonneuve monument stands before the neo-Classical Banque de Montréal.

tower holds a carillon of ten bells, while the western contains the 11 000kg (24 000lb) Gros Bourdon bell. The **Chapelle du Sacré-Coeur** (Sacred Heart Chapel) behind the altar was severely damaged by fire in 1978, and was reconstructed in contemporary style, with striking bronze panels and light oak finishing.

Next door to the basilica is the **Vieux Séminaire de Saint-Sulpice★** (Old Sulpician Seminary), the oldest building still standing on the island of Montreal. Constructed between 1684 and 1687, with later extensions, in its day this was more than a center of spiritual

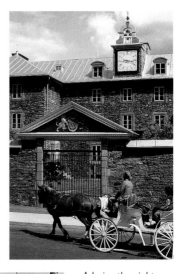

Admire the sights — such as one of the oldest clocks in North America, on the Old Sulpician Seminary — from the comfort of a calèche.

The imposing twin towers of Notre Dame Basilica are undaunted by surrounding skyscrapers.

23

learning. The Sulpicians ran the island of Montreal as feudal masters for 200 years. The clock, dating from 1701, is one of the oldest in the USA and Canada.

Glance down lanes and alleys, and you'll catch a glimpse of **gardens of reflection**. These green spaces are oases in the city, one of the legacies of Church ownership of urban land and favorable tax status.

On the north side of Place d'Armes stands the domed **Banque de Montréal★** (Bank of Montreal) building, with its neo-Classical façade, designed in part by the firm of McKim, Mead and White. The exterior grandeur and lavish spaces inside made it a secular temple of British and Protestant power during the growth of Montreal. The design acted as something of a trademark, copied in the bank's branches elsewhere. Inside, the **museum** of banknotes and banking is open to the public.

Just down the street is the **Banque Royale du Canada★** (Royal Bank of Canada), at 360 St-Jacques West, the tallest structure in the British Empire when it was erected in 1928. It has an ornate Renaissance lobby and bronze decoration, with a magnificent marble staircase leading to the huge banking hall.

From Place d'Armes, you can hire a horse-drawn **calèche** (carriage) to continue your tour along the cobblestone streets of the old city, an experience that exactly suits the era of your surroundings. Additional calèches await in front of the Old Port, on Rue de la Commune.

Walk two blocks eastward to reach Montreal's stone-clad **Hôtel de Ville★** (City Hall) (DY), at 275 Notre-Dame East, erected between 1872 and 1878. The mansard roof is typical of the Second Empire style used widely in public buildings and residences at the time; the oversized windows and ceilings bespeak power. Perhaps the most notable event here was a speech by Charles de Gaulle in 1967, in which he called out 'Vive le Québec Libre' (Long Live Free Quebec), and fanned the flames of secession (*open Mon-Fri 8.30am-4.30pm for guided tours*).

To the north, behind City Hall, is the open expanse of the **Champ de Mars** (DY), a military exercise ground under the French régime, and now a sunning and picnicking spot for office workers on pleasant days. Running through the site are parallel ridges of stone, all that remains of the original fortifications of the city (*see* p.9).

Just west of City Hall is the **Vieux Palais de Justice** (Old Court House), pre-dating City Hall (1856) in a more modest neo-Classical style, complete with pediment. The dome and top floor are later additions. Adjoining, to the west (1 Notre-Dame East), is the newer court house, a black tower. And across the way, at 100 Notre-Dame East, is the **Ernest Cormier** building, dating from 1925, and also originally

Take an unfogrettable ride back into the 19C in a calèche, the cobblestones of Rue de la Commune and Rue St-Paul resounding to the clip-clop of horseshoes.

used for the courts. The building was renamed after its designer, Canada's most distinguished architect in the first half of the 20C. The use of Classical orders, with a colonnade at the base, is notable. The building now houses a school of music and drama.

Nelson's Column and City Hall stand on one side of the lively Place Jacques-Cartier.

While you're in the area, call in at **Infotouriste**, the local tourist information service, at 174 Notre-Dame East. Brochures and maps are available here for Old Montreal and the entire city.

Historic Houses

At 280 Notre-Dame East, set back along a gravelled drive, is **Château Ramezay★** (DY), the mansion erected for governor Claude de

Ramezay in 1705, and used as headquarters by the first British administrators. The restored chateau now houses a **museum**, with a collection of artifacts depicting life on Montreal island, dating from before French colonization, and a major collection of early Canadian art (*open June-Sept daily 10am-6pm, Oct-May Tues-Sun 10am-4.30pm*).

A couple of blocks beyond, at 450 Notre-Dame East, the **Sir George-Étienne Cartier Historic Site★**, a set of Second-Empire homes that were inhabited by Sir George-Étienne Cartier, one of the founders of the Canadian confederation in 1867, and a proponent of rapprochement between the founding peoples. One of the houses has been restored to reflect life in Victorian times, while the other is a museum devoted to Cartier's life and work (*open May-Aug daily, April-May and Sept-late Dec Wed-Sun*).

Street Life

Returning to City Hall, turn southward to look down the wide cobbled pedestrian street and gardens sloping gently toward the St Lawrence River. This is **Place Jacques-Cartier★★**, dating from 1804, its signature column a monument to Lord Nelson (DY 2). Pause to admire the

Step back in time to the 18C at the Château Ramezay museum.

panorama of the river and harbor, the cafés, the *terrasses* extending out from stone-clad buildings, and the public gardens of **Place de la Dauversière** (DY 14) extending to the east. Once a public market, Place Jacques-Cartier is one of the most lively, attractive squares in Old Montreal, with its flower sellers, café-sitters, jugglers, photographers, magicians and itinerant artists. Few can resist the lure of the street cafés in such a pleasant setting, for a drink, a light snack or a meal. Not even winter puts a damper on the activities – crowds gather here to welcome in the New Year.

Experience the burst of spring in Place Jacques-Cartier, where floral displays seem to imply that winter never existed, and jugglers, caricaturists and magicians celebrate the season.

19C Panorama

Refreshed and rested, walk down Place Jacques-Cartier, cross to the gardens along Rue de la Commune, and turn towards the north. Spread before you is a sweeping vista of a virtually intact 19C Montreal, stretching along the waterfront. Buildings are two, three and four storeys tall, stone-clad or revealing the wrought-iron skeletons of the most avant-garde technology of the day. Painted signs announce

ship chandlers, and swinging doors lead to passageways from the cobbled thoroughfare to former stable yards. Of course, the travel agencies, bicycle-rental shops, and other more contemporary businesses in these premises are a sign of the times.

Turn eastward along Rue de la Commune to the impressive, long, neo-Classical building stretching a full block, with the central silver dome that served as a landmark for sailors approaching from the harbor. **Marché Bonsecours★** (Bonsecours Market) (DY) (350 St-Paul East, with a waterfront entrance as well), dating from 1849, has served the public in a succession of functions, originally as a great public exchange of goods and produce on two cavernous floors. It has also been a city hall, concert auditorium, and, for a time, the temporary seat of government of United Canada, after the unpleasantness of rioting and the burning of the legislature on Place d'Youville (*see* p.11).

Turbulence and brute commerce are in the past. Today's market has been restored and updated as a performance, retail and exhibition space. Go up to the great gallery, check out the current exhibition, and browse the boutiques displaying fine fabrics, Inuit carvings and reproductions of period wooden furniture.

Just east of the market, and dwarfed by it, is the **Chapelle Notre-Dame-de-Bonsecours★**. Regarded as the sailors' church of Montreal, its construction started in 1771. Look for the votive offerings left by seamen hung in the chapel, and the paintings on fitted boards of wood, by F E Meloche, dating from the end of the 19C. Below the chapel lay the foundations of the first stone church in Montreal, built by Sister Marguerite Bourgeoys, a legendary figure in the early history of the city, who is

Let the bustle of Place Jacques-Cartier entertain you while you refresh yourself at one of the many street cafés on the square.

The chapel built within the steeple of Chapelle Notre-Dame-de-Bonsecours offers fine views over the port and St Lawrence River.

Opposite the Chapelle Notre-Dame-de-Bonsecours, housing Sister Marguerite Bourgeoys Museum, is the 18C Maison du Calvet.

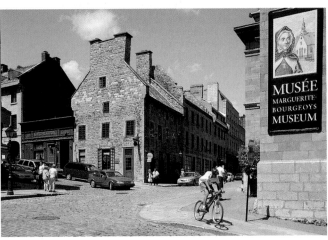

commemorated here by a small **museum**. Climb the hundred or so steps to the 'aerial chapel' and take in the panoramic **view★** over the St Lawrence, the Old Port and St Helen's Island.

A block up, narrow **Rue St-Paul★★**, one of the oldest streets in Montreal, is lined with attractive 19C stone houses that remain from the French régime, with characteristic steep-pitched roofs to shed heavy snow loads. One of the finest examples of these traditional residences is **Maison du Calvet★** (at the corner of Rue Bonsecours), one-time home of Pierre du Calvet, a Huguenot who supported the American Revolution.

The Original Harbor

Walk back out onto Rue de la Commune, on the waterfront, and look ahead towards the water. Straight in front of you lies the original port of Montreal.

Beyond the modern breakwater, in the main channel of the river, are the **Sainte Marie Rapids**, the first of a series of rapids stretching to Lachine that made further navigation upriver treacherous, and reinforced Montreal's position as a terminus for ocean-going ships.

Thrills and a thorough soaking are both guaranteed when jet boating on the Lachine rapids.

The area all around was subject to flooding every spring into the 19C. You can ride the rapids – an exciting but wet experience (*see* p.125).

Off to the right (west), at an arching steel bridge leading into the cargo terminus, is a set of locks at the opening of the **Lachine Canal**. Opened in 1825, the canal provided easy passage around the rapids for boats laden with goods, and spurred the development of the Canadian west. Along its banks grew the first industrial district in Canada. Today, a cycling path runs alongside the canal to the suburb of Lachine, about 12km (7.5 miles) away.

Cruise ships use the original port area, while petroleum carriers and container ships dock elsewhere on the river these days. On the far side of the river is the **St Lawrence Seaway** for ocean-going ships, which made the Lachine Canal obsolete.

New life has been breathed into the piers in the Old Port.

Le Vieux-Port★ (The Old Port)

Most of what stands before you is a once-abandoned area of piers and sheds (DY), recycled into a year-round complex of entertainment, recreation and education about the port itself, complete with cycle paths, gardens, amusements and exhibitions. In summer the esplanade is ideal for walking, cycling or skating, and has fine **views★** over the port.

Rue de la Commune, alongside the Old Port, is a good place to catch a **calèche** (horse-drawn carriage) for a ride around this part of town, if you haven't already done so. Otherwise, continue right into the vast waterside park – it doesn't cost a penny to enter, though there are nominal fees for activities inside. Trams carry visitors from one end to the other, with a running commentary on the port's history. Bicycles may be rented to

Right: Costumed pipers entertain strollers on the seafront.

use on-site, or to continue down the bike path along the Lachine Canal, or you can hire a pedal boat in summer.

Start your exploration at the **Tour de l'Horloge** (Clock Tower), at the north-east end. It was erected in 1922 in memory of merchant mariners lost in World War I. Climb to the top – 192 steps – for a view of the water, and back over Old Montreal.

Recent exhibitions and activities at the Old Port have included ones dealing with the sinkings of the *Titanic* and *Empress of Ireland* (largely with artifacts from the latter); a permanent **flea market** in a cavernous shed; a gigantic **maze** to the taste of most children; the **Interactive Science Centre**; and the **IMAX** super-screen cinema (look for listings in the newspapers). Discount coupons for Old Port activities are widely available. Ask at your hotel or at one of the Infotouriste offices.

Ferries operate in the warmer months to

The Interactive Science Centre is a magnet for youngsters.

Longueuil, on the south shore of the river, and to the park and casino on **Île Sainte-Hélène** (St Helen's Island), as do **harbor cruises★** and jet boat trips on the Lachine rapids (*see* pp.31 and 125). In any given summer, the Old Port might be the venue for a comedy festival, a circus (*Cirque du Soleil* in spring, every even-numbered year), or concerts. In winter, skating and rides on inflatable tubes are on offer, along with a nativity scene featuring live actors.

From the Old Port head westward. You can go back along Rue de la Commune, or, for a change of view, cross back onto the meandering **Rue St-Paul★★**, a block to the north. St-Paul here is lined with ex-warehouses, now converted to boutiques, photo shops, a **doll museum** (105 St-Paul East), fine restaurants, night clubs, galleries and souvenir shops. Crowds overflow onto the cobblestones every night during the warmer months. If you're touring during the day, this is a good

The Tour de l'Horloge offers great views across the port to Old Montreal.

place to take a break for anything from a snack to a complete meal.

Six blocks west of Place Jacques-Cartier is **Place Royale** (DZ), a small square, the site of the first public gathering place and market in Montreal. To the north is **L'Ancienne Douane** (Old Customs House) (150 St-Paul West), dating from 1838. It is one of the first British public structures, in a neo-Classical style that would have fitted well in the London of the day.

Just to the west and south of the square is a triangle of land known as the **Pointe-à-Callière**, fronted by the sleek prow of the **Musée d'Archéologie et d'Histoire de Montréal**★★ (Montreal Museum of Archaeology and History). The striking modern Éperon Building is directly above the site where Montreal was founded. The museum continues right down into the foundations of the original buildings with an underground section which runs along the former bed of the St Pierre River, through the **archaeological crypt** under Place Royale,

The Montreal Museum of Archaeology and History is built on the site where the original colony was founded, Pointe-à-Callière.

and ending up across the way in the Old Customs House, where exhibits of Montreal's commercial past are displayed. Aside from the path into the past, the museum exhibits artifacts from the French régime and from indigenous times, and models of Place Royale over the centuries; offers a multimedia presentation; and encompasses the first electrically operated pumping station in the city. The **restaurant** on the top floor, accessible without payment of the museum admission fee, serves excellent, reasonably priced meals in a space flooded with natural light, and affords some of the best **views**★ of the port area.

Continue westward along **Place d'Youville**★ (CDZ), a wide cobbled way, unpretentious, placid and charming, bordered by stone-clad and iron-framed buildings from the 19C, former stables and warehouses, now turned into offices and residential condominiums. The square covers what used to be the St Pierre River. Along the south side of the square are the so-called **Écuries d'Youville** (Youville Stables), granaries built in the early 19C for the Grey Nuns, now housing offices and a restaurant. At Rue St-Pierre is a section of the **Hôpital Général des Sœurs Grises** (Grey Nuns Hospital), dating from the 17C.

An old fire station set in the middle of Place d'Youville (no 335) now serves as the **Centre d'Histoire de Montréal**★ (Montreal History Center) (CZ), with treasured photographs and re-creations of a 1940s residence, a factory floor, and even an old streetcar. The museum also offers walking tours in French of Montreal neighborhoods (☎ **514 872 3207** for information and opening times).

Just south of Place d'Youville, at 118 Rue St-Pierre, is the **Musée Marc-Aurèle Fortin**★ (DZ), a museum dedicated to the painter who established Quebec's own landscape style in the 20C.

Place d'Youville ends at Rue McGill, an easy
route to follow if you care to head back north
and up the escarpment to downtown. Along
the way are workaday office blocks dating from
the early 20C, and some excellent restaurants
that cater to executives in the financial district.
Boris Bistro, 465 McGill at St-Paul, is a good
choice (leg of duck or braised rabbit, about
$20).

Victoria Square (CZ), at Rue St-Jacques,
anchors the western end of the financial
district. Bordering it is the **Centre de
Commerce Mondial** (World Trade Center, *see*
p.125), which integrates a modern office tower
with the intact façades of 19C buildings. The
glassed-in courtyard, complete with fountains
and benches, is a gentrification of an urban
alley, Ruelle des Fortifications. The interior
street makes for a pleasant stroll and rest stop
in any season.

West of the World Trade Center is the **Tour
de la Bourse★** (Stock Exchange Tower), 800
Victoria Square. The trading floor is open to
visitors, but is more tame than exchanges
elsewhere. Across Rue St-Antoine, at the corner
of Rue University, the building with the curving
façade is the headquarters of the **International
Civil Aviation Organization** (ICAO), a United
Nations agency, one of a number of
international organizations attracted by
Montreal's multilingual population, amenities,
and generally low cost of living. Underneath is
the **suburban bus station** serving communities
on the south shore of the St Lawrence River
opposite Montreal.

From Victoria Square metro station, catch a
train to continue onward. Or continue on foot
underground: Victoria Square marks the
southernmost tip of the Underground City,
Montreal's system of sheltered pedestrian ways
and concourses (*see* p.58).

*The Sun Life
Building on
Dorchester Square,
the largest building
in its time, is now
overshadowed by
modern skyscrapers.*

DOWNTOWN

Montreal moved uphill in the 19C, and went upscale as well, as it evolved from a port of entry into a complex urban center of commerce, manufacturing and services.

While not immune to suburbanization, Montreal is quite different from many North American cities. The great majority of Montrealers live in apartments and are not totally dependent on the car. Flocking to where others are is in the culture, and Montreal has managed to keep a vibrant central area, busy – and safe – at most hours of the day and night.

A good place to start your look at the

modern city is at the corner of Boulevard
Maisonneuve and Peel (*metro:* Peel) (AZ).
Office towers dating from the 1920s and 1930s
form a canyon to the east, looking somewhat
like New York on a reduced scale. Right down
at street level, local tastes predominate. There
are McDonald's restaurants and a Burger King,
but also numerous places at which to stop for a
croissant and coffee, a sandwich or baguette.

Around Dorchester Square★

The **Dominion Square Building★**, at 1010
Sainte-Catherine, dating from 1929 and in the
Renaissance Revival style, is one of the finer
buildings, with clearly demarcated base, central
and top sections, as well as insets to bring light
inside. The indoor shops were an innovation in
their day, and a precursor of later development
styles.

Walk south on Peel just a half-
block, and you'll come to
Dorchester Square★ (BZ),
formerly Dominion Square.
Under any name (Lord
Dorchester was an early British
proponent of protecting French
Canadian rights), the square is
green and leafy, extending across
Boulevard René-Lévesque to the
equally large Place du Canada.
Dorchester Square is the site of
an early 19C Catholic cemetery, where many of
the victims of the 1832 cholera epidemic were
buried. A statue of Sir John A Macdonald
(BZ 5), first prime minister of confederated
Canada, looks over the scene. Other monuments
honour poet Robert Burns (BZ 8), Canada's
contribution to the Boer War and Queen
Victoria (in the form of a jubilee lion) (BZ 7).

Almost every visitor to Montreal stops by
Dorchester Square at some point. Tour **buses**

*Pick up a city tour
bus from Dorchester
Square.*

depart from the back of the Dominion Square Building, on the square. On the ground floor of the same building, facing the square, is **Centre Infotouriste**, the main tourist information office, dispensing not just information, flyers and booklets about Montreal, but also selling tours, books and souvenirs, and providing most travel services through partner companies.

Southward around Dorchester Square and Place du Canada spreads a panorama of significant buildings. Facing the east side, at 1155 Metcalfe, is the **Sun Life Building★★**, largest in the British Empire when it was opened in 1918. Classic, columned, massive and suitably imposing, it kept European gold reserves in safekeeping during the Second World War.

On the opposite side of the park, along Peel,

Sir John A Macdonald gazes out over Dorchester Square.

a surviving wing of the former **Windsor Hotel★** has been converted to tasteful office space. The huge Second-Empire mansard is notable, but unfortunately the ornate interior space is not open to visitors.

Basilique-Cathédrale Marie-Reine-du-Monde★★ (Mary Queen of the World Cathedral) faces Boulevard René-Lévesque just west of Dorchester Square, a reduced but still-massive version of St Peter's in Rome, right down to the magnificent baldachin (interior canopy). Statues of the patron saints of Montreal's parishes stand all along the roof.

To the east and west along René-Lévesque are some of Montreal's newer and taller office towers. The **Laurentian Building** (BZ) is 'sliced' diagonally at the corner of Peel, a reference to how the roofs of Montreal row houses have traditionally marked intersections. To the north across the boulevard is the steel tower of the **Canadian Imperial Bank of Commerce**,

The Basilique-Cathédrale Marie-Reine-du-Monde has resolutely survived a tumultuous past of bombardment and reconstruction.

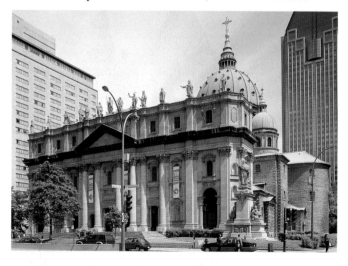

with incongruous slate-filled panels. The **IBM Marathon Building** (or **Le 1250 René-Lévesque**), at the corner of Drummond, is known for its curving east façade. Sheathed in grey granite, it breaks its continuous surfaces with a variety of architectural conceits, including projecting prows and grilles.

On the exterior of these and other contemporary buildings, much of what appears to be cladding of tinted glass is actually polished aluminium, covering plentiful insulation – a method of construction particularly suited to the climate.

Around Rue de la Gauchetière

The traditional meets the modern – the IBM Marathon Building towers over St George's Anglican Church.

Follow Rue Peel as it slopes down the escarpment that runs the length of Montreal island. At the corner of Rue de la Gauchetière, the next street, is **St George's Anglican Church★** (BZ), a fine neo-Gothic structure with detailed interior woodwork, set back amid trees

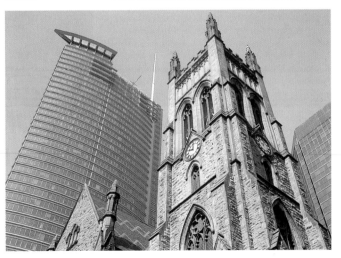

Take to the ice at the Atrium, the domed rink at 1000 de la Gauchetière.

The massive Windsor Station was once the departure point for many a journey across the continent.

and gardens behind a wrought-iron fence, as if it were set in an English country town.

Across La Gauchetière is **Windsor Station★**, constructed in Romanesque Revival style, and opened in 1889. Massive and beautifully detailed, it was once the departure point for transcontinental Canadian Pacific trains. Now quiet for much of the day, it's worth entering to admire the grand interior space.

Just west of the station, and in total contrast, is the **Molson Centre**, a functional red-brick, steel and aluminium casing for the arena and assorted systems that it contains. The Molson Centre is home of the legendary Canadiens hockey team, and also a venue for musical performances and even massive theatrical presentations.

Walk back east a couple of blocks, and under the pedestrian overpass. The building at **1000 de la Gauchetière** is one of the tallest in the city's skyline. Go inside and take a look at the **Atrium**, the domed rink that satisfies the urge to ice skate of locals and visitors year-round.

Eastward on La Gauchetière, on the south side at Rue Mansfield, is the massive, rippled concrete exterior of **Place Bonaventure**, a large exhibition and convention area, also housing shopping arcades and the Hilton Hotel.

(A turn to the right past Place Bonaventure, and down the hill, brings you to Victoria Square and the Financial district, end-point of the route through Old Montreal.)

To continue your exploration of downtown you need to turn to the north where across La Gauchetière, opposite Place Bonaventure, you'll see the rather unpromising garage entrance labelled **Gare Centrale** (Central Station) (BZ). Plunge inside anyway, along the interior sidewalk, and through the glass doors. You'll find yourself in the great main concourse (106m/350ft long, 10m/33ft high, opened in 1943). Bas-relief murals in Art Deco style show scenes of industry, agriculture and recreation across the country. Every detail is

pregnant with the significance of the role of the Canadian National Railroad in uniting Canada. Indeed, the national anthem is emblazoned in both official languages.

The concourse and the shops and pathways just to the north are the busiest neighborhood of Montreal's **Underground City★★★** (*see* p.58). Just north of the main hall are cheery passages lined with bakeries, sausage shops, German-style beer halls and full-service restaurants. Chairs and tables set outside are often crowded with patrons, just as at any sidewalk café, except that the weather never makes a difference. This is a good place to take a break. Most of the points mentioned below can be reached by underground passages, as well as along surface streets.

Office workers blend with shoppers and visitors on the Terrasse, Place Ville-Marie.

Just north of Central Station is the **Queen Elizabeth Hotel**, on Boulevard René-Lévesque. Austere, grey and dull on the outside, it is a comfortable up-market establishment inside, and after 40 years, still one of the largest hotels in the city, with more than a thousand rooms. Jutting out is an elevator shaft that provides panoramas on the way up to the rooms. John Lennon and Yoko Ono wrote *Give Peace a Chance* during a love-in on the premises in 1969. Montreal's Beaver Club, traditional gathering area for English-speaking nabobs, is here too.

On the north side of René-Lévesque are the cruciform towers of **Place Ville-Marie**★★ (BZ), the signature office complex that set Montreal as the forerunner of urban design when it opened in the early 1960s. While hardly a religious edifice, the form reflects the cross on Mount Royal and the city's coat of arms. The **Tour Banque Royale**★ (Royal Bank Tower), designed by I M Pei, dominates the complex. Place Ville-Marie pioneered the concept of sheltered concourses of shops and services connecting to adjacent hubs, such as Central Station. Above ground, it was the first office center to blur the divisions between sidewalk and private property, inviting the public into plazas, to continue inside through a variety of entry points.

East along René-Lévesque, at Rue St-Alexandre, is **St Patrick's Basilica**, a Gothic-style church opened in 1847, set back from the street in attractive gardens. The carved oak panelling and pine columns are

Uncompromising design at the Tour Banque Royale, Place Ville-Marie.

especially notable. St Patrick's has traditionally served the Irish community.

Shopping District

Return northward to Rue Sainte-Catherine on Metcalfe or University, or by strolling underground. **Rue Sainte-Catherine** (BZ) is the busiest pedestrian thoroughfare in Canada. Of course, there's vehicular traffic as well, which jaywalking pedestrians never respect, creating a continuing rodeo of braking and screeching. Local drivers know what to expect, and injuries are rare, but visitors are cautioned not to imitate the ways of the fleet-footed Montréalais.

The traditional La Baie department store, with the modern Place Montréal Trust beyond.

Look eastward and westward to some of the larger stores: Ogilvy, Simons, La Baie (known as The Bay, or Hudson's Bay Company, elsewhere). Less obvious are some of the multi-levelled indoor shopping courses reaching above and below street level. The **Eaton Centre** at the corner of McGill College Avenue, organized around an atrium, houses retailers with familiar names like Gap, together with more up-market European and local marques,

Your first stroll on Rue Sainte-Catherine reveals a disarming combination of North American skyscrapers and efficiency, and Gallic fashion, flair and spirit.

as well as cinemas and eateries. After dark the thoroughfare takes on a new life as the bars, clubs and nightspots spring into action.

Across McGill College, **Place Montréal Trust★★** is the most massive of the newer skyscrapers of Montreal, clad in pink marble and blue-tinted glass and aluminum, its volumes intersecting like so many Lego blocks. The lower floors house a city of boutiques, restaurants and eateries; the central plaza holds one of the highest indoor jets of water in the world.

Opposite La Baie, at the corner of Sainte-Catherine and Union Avenue, is **Phillips**

Looking along McGill College Avenue, with Place Montréal Trust skyscraper on the left and Mount Royal in the distance.

Square, the only open green space in the immediate area, crowded with vendors in the warmer months. Just to the west is **Birks**, an upscale jewelry emporium, as well known locally as is Tiffany's in New York. Gaze at the window displays and dream …

Place Montréal Trust shopping concourse.

Fur District

A block to the north (BY), around Boulevard de Maisonneuve and Rue Bleury, is the fur district, where the business that built Montreal carries on. Nine out of ten Canadian fur coats are handcrafted in workshops in several commercial buildings. The workshops welcome potential customers, and may be visited on tours that explain the sorting and processing of furs, and the sewing of garments.

Eastward, Sainte-Catherine is somewhat humdrum, continuing to Place des Arts (*see* p.60). But of some interest is the curious **St James United Church**. The largest Protestant church in the city, with a glorious Gothic façade, it fell on hard times in the 1900s as its parishioners moved out of the central area. Commercial buildings were erected where the church lawn once stood, obscuring the view of the building, but providing much-needed revenue, as well as rather unusual decorative details in some of the newly created offices and upstairs shops. If time permits, pop into the church, offices or shops to have a look.

More conventional, at least in appearance, is **Christ Church Cathedral★** (BZ), at the corner of University, another fine Gothic structure that dates from 1859. Its spire of textured metal replaces a problematic stone original. This church solved its financial woes by selling off rights to the space below, and sat on massive stilts for several years while **Les Promenades de la Cathédrale** shopping complex was excavated and finished off.

Who would guess that below Christ Church Cathedral lies the bustling 100-shop complex of Les Promenades de la Cathédrale?

Above ground, there are no visible signs of the subterranean commerce, save for entry kiosks placed to either side of the church. On the northern part of the property is **La Place de la Cathédrale★** office tower, reflecting the cathedral not only in its mirrored surface, but through such features as a vast entry hall and peaked roof.

Walk back along Sainte-Catherine. Along Rue Peel to the north is **Les Cours Mont-Royal** (ABZ), where you'll find the sedate and pricey premises of retailers of clothes and furnishings, as well as the grand Égyptien cinema. Way up in the atrium, under the skylight, are *tingmiluks*, Inuit birdman sculptures.

Glance up other side streets. Each is a neighborhood in itself. Rue de la Montagne is home to some fine small hotels. Crescent and Bishop streets, north of Sainte-Catherine, are lined with typical Montreal attached greystone townhouses, originally three stories tall, now stretched, renovated and transformed into bars, clubs and fine restaurants, but still showing their original character. To the south the streets are more mixed, with some nightclubs and restaurants, and an odd surviving private club and a mansion or two, with curving entrance drive, providing variety.

McGill Area

Return to wide McGill College Avenue, a truncated boulevard, and walk northward from Sainte-Catherine. Pause at 1981 McGill College, at the **Banque Nationale de Paris★** building (Tour BNP) to gaze (as everybody does) at the sculpture, *The Illuminated Crowd* (AZ 12), by Raymond Mason, showing a lively mix of comic-strip humans moulded in polymers. The 'blue building', as it is affectionately called by locals after its blue glass exterior, joins with, and preserves, a row of greystone townhouses that might otherwise have been demolished.

McGill College leads to the gates of the prestigious **McGill University★** (AY), and points to the ever-present 'Mountain' (Mount Royal). The original college was endowed by fur tycoon James McGill early in the 19C. Take a few minutes, at least, to walk through the gates, and admire buildings set on the edge of the central lawns. Few campuses occupy such valuable real estate in the heart of downtown. Notable at the far end of the entry drive is Moyse Hall, a Victorian structure. The **Redpath Museum of Natural History★**, to the left, has an extensive collection, including preserved animals and mineral specimens, and an Egyptian mummy (*open weekdays and Sunday afternoons; closed Fridays in summer*).

Additional McGill buildings fronting on Rue Sherbrooke include **Pollock Hall** (555 Sherbrooke West), a concert venue, and the **Musée McCord d'Histoire Canadienne★★**

Depicting the human condition, The Illuminated Crowd sculpture stands out against the 'blue building', the Tour BNP.

(McCord Museum of Canadian History, 690 Sherbrooke West) (ABY), a treasure house of costumes, textiles and artifacts of the peoples of Canada, including Native Americans (Indians) and Inuit. This important collection comprises over 100 000 exhibits, many donated by David Ross McCord in 1919, and was originally housed in the greystone McGill Union Building. Unfortunately, even the recent extension and renovation has not provided enough space for more than a part of the collection to be shown at any one time. The **Notman Archives** is an outstanding collection of some 700 000 prints and plates.

Golden Square Mile

The stretch of **Rue Sherbrooke★** running west from McGill University speaks of money, and plenty of it. It's the main thoroughfare of Montreal's traditional Golden Square Mile, where fur traders and railroad barons built their mansions. Some of the graceful residences on Sherbrooke and nearby streets remain as banks, corporate headquarters, charitable foundations, and foreign missions. The **Alcan Building★** (AZ), at 1188 Sherbrooke West, is a sleek structure that showcases the metal produced by its namesake company as it reaches out over an interior courtyard to a one-time hotel.

The **Church of St Andrew and St Paul**, at the corner of Bishop, served the Scottish among the barons, McGill, McTavish and McKay being prominent names. The dour temple is completely of stone on the inside, with an immense stained-glass window above the main altar.

Mainstays of the upper classes today – bilingual and of more diverse origin – include the **Holt Renfrew** department store at the corner of Mountain (Rue de la Montagne),

The contrasting architectural styles of the elegant mansions on Rue Sherbrooke West are a legacy of the area's wealthy past.

and the most elegant **Ritz Carlton Hotel★**, at the corner of Drummond, with fine detailing both in the Renaissance-style façade and in the interior woodwork. Former and future prime ministers patronize the dining room. Lunch inside, and brunch in the Ritz garden in season, are elegant, impeccable and fun.

Musée des Beaux-Arts de Montréal★★ (Montreal Museum of Fine Arts)

Next to the Church of St Andrew and St Paul, at the corner of Du Musée on both sides of Sherbrooke, is the **Musée des Beaux-Arts de Montréal★★** (Montreal Museum of Fine Arts). The newer, contemporary-style section on the south side of the street (Desmarais Pavilion), designed by Moshe Safdie, subsumes the shell of what used to be an apartment building on the site. This section holds the collection of European art, modern art and temporary exhibitions. (It is recommended to use the elevator once inside, rather than the treacherous stairs.)

The original Classical-style Bennaiah Gibb Pavilion across Sherbrooke, accessible by a tunnel where a collection of ancient art is displayed, houses the permanent collection. Included are the works of luminaries of Canadian art, including the Group of Seven, Cornélius Krieghoff, Jean-Paul Riopelle, and local artists Paul-Émile Borduas and James Wilson Morrice. Also notable is the collection of Native American and Inuit art works.

Take a short detour here along **Rue Crescent★** (AZ), a street of charming Victorian buildings housing galleries, boutiques and restaurants which spill out onto the pavements in summer. Also the heart of the club and bar scene, the area throbs on into the early hours.

At 2200 Rue Crescent is an annex to the Museum of Fine Arts, designed by Frank Gehry, and housing the **Musée des Arts Décoratifs de Montréal★** (Montreal Museum of Decorative Arts), dedicated to 20C design in textiles, graphics and objects from the home and office.

Back on Rue Sherbrooke, near the museum,

Colourful, vibrant and full of charm – the essence of Rue Crescent.

are numerous private art galleries specializing variously in Inuit, contemporary Canadian, and European and American art. To the west, past Rue Guy, commercial use gives way to apartment blocks, but only on the south side. The hillside to the north, behind the great stone walls, holds the venerable buildings of the **Grand Séminaire de Montréal** (Sulpician Seminary), where priests are trained on a peaceful urban estate. Two 'witches' hat' towers, notably French in design, remain from early fortifications on the site, and are among the oldest structures in the city. The **chapel★** is especially impressive.

Other Museums

South of the gallery and museum area, along Boulevard de Maisonneuve, are the office-type buildings that house the downtown campus of **Concordia University** (AZ).The library, along Rue Bishop, incorporates the richly detailed Beaux-Arts façade of a razed apartment building. The **Ellen Art Gallery**, 1400 De Maisonneuve West, devoted to Canadian art, is associated with the university (*closed Sun*).

The **Centre Canadien d'Architecture★** (Canadian Center for Architecture, 1920 Rue Baile) is an ensemble of curving, plain masonry enfolding the painstakingly restored Shaughnessy House. Founded by architect-philanthropist Phyllis Lambert, it invites visitors to discover all aspects of building as an art as well as trade, and provides a library and base for scholars of architecture. The focus is usually on a current exhibition, rather than the permanent collection. Across Boulevard René-Lévesque is the unusual **CCA Architectural Garden** on a plot of land isolated by expressway ramps, its sculptures suggestive of structures existing, lost, or yet to be built (*closed Mon all year, and also Tues Oct-May*).

The Underground City★★★

Montreal exists on the surface as a conventional city, and below as a series of ultramodern subterranean shopping arcades and passages connecting with metro stations, hotels and even public services such as libraries. It's quite possible to awaken in a hotel, have breakfast, go off to a meeting, continue to the office, and finish with dinner and a movie, without ever stepping outside. Whether the temperature is in the 90s°F (30°C), or 22°F below zero (-30°C), whether the streets are piled with a foot (30 cm) of snow or awash in a thunderstorm, makes no difference.

As in any more conventional city, there are neighborhoods, some of them upscale, some more workaday, some staid, and some bristling with excitement. Not all the areas of Montreal's Underground City interconnect, but the network advances steadily from year to year. And like any conventional city, it constantly undergoes renovation and faces controversy over design and planning.

Critics have repeatedly claimed that the Underground City shuts out natural light and a sense of contact with the greater world – something like a Las Vegas casino. So light wells were added to Place Ville-Marie a couple of years ago. Then critics complained that the pure lines of the plaza above were spoiled. You can't win them all, but the Underground City itself is a winner, attracting more than a quarter of a million passersby every working day.

The senior sector in the network is **Place Ville-Marie** – a bold experiment in its infancy in the 1960s. Oddly enough, Place Ville-Marie recently revolutionized its revolution with an interior makeover that opened additional outside access directly to businesses.

The network continues southward under the **Queen Elizabeth Hotel** to the most lively area, the ever-busy shops and boutiques in **Gare Centrale** (Central Station). Onward it flows to nearby **Place Bonaventure** exhibition hall and metro station, and **Gare Windsor** (Windsor Station) and its commuter trains. A connecting parallel section runs south along Côte du Beaver Hall (Beaver Hall Hill) from Boulevard René-Lévesque to the suburban bus station, **Stock**

Exchange Tower, and the **World Trade Center**.

Northward from Place Ville-Marie, passageways run up to Rue Sherbrooke, and snake to the east and west, joining the sedate and pricey **Cours Mont-Royal** shopping galleries on Rue Peel, with condos upstairs, to the cavernous **Place Montréal Trust** (descending several stories underground and rising several stories above), to the **Eaton Centre** at McGill College Avenue, to the shopping grottoes of **Les Promenades de la Cathédrale**, and finally, to **La Baie** department store. A northward branch from **Place de la Cathédrale** dog-legs to end at the McCord Museum on Rue Sherbrooke.

Additional parallel cities lie to the east and west. **Place des Arts** connects under Rue Sainte-Catherine to the tiered arcades and entertainment spaces of **Complexe Desjardins**, which in turn joins the shops and offices of **Complexe Guy-Favreau** across René-Lévesque, and the **Palais des Congrès** (Convention Center) that hulks over the Ville Marie Expressway.

Far less ambitious, but still comforting if you're walking, are the interconnecting passageways around the **bus station** in the Latin Quarter in the east end; and the connected shopping and residential complexes of **Place Alexis Nihon** and **Westmount Square** on the western edge of downtown.

The Eaton Centre.

EASTERN DOWNTOWN

Unlike the older, central downtown area, which grew at a measured pace, the eastern edge contains several contiguous mega-developments, dating from the 1960s and 1970s, when the urban planning style was to transform neighborhoods in one fell swoop. The result is private and public spaces in familiar concrete, but with a Latin touch of lively plazas and the trademark Montreal four-season accessibility.

Place des Arts★★

Place des Arts★★ (BY), starting from the corner of Sainte-Catherine and Jeanne-Mance streets, is the city's main cultural center and covers several former city blocks, with performance venues, rehearsal suites and affiliated fine arts establishments, all connected by above-ground plazas, and a great sheltered concourse that features shops and eating places.

Salle Wilfrid-Pelletier is the major concert hall, at the northern edge of the complex (always approach from the south, under the plaza), home to the Orchestre Symphonique (Montreal Symphony Orchestra) and site of performances by visiting stars. Performance halls range in size down to **Théâtre Maisonneuve** and the intimate **Théâtre Café de la Place**.

Stretching along Jeanne-Mance on the western side of Place des Arts is the stark, columned but otherwise impenetrable wall of the **Musée d'Art Contemporain de Montréal★★** (Montreal Museum of Modern Art). Once again, enter from the east. About 6 000 works are in the permanent collection, dating from 1939 onwards, and displayed in light and airy galleries. The emphasis is on Canadian art, with a particular focus on Quebec artists such

The Salle Wilfrid-Pelletier concert hall stands on the north side of the vast Place des Arts complex.

Turn from visitor to celebrant during a summer festival, when the streets around Place des Arts become stages for jazz, African beats, comedy and buskers.

as Paul-Émile Borduas, Jean-Paul Riopelle, David Moore and Alfred Pellan. International artists are also represented in the permanent collection and temporary exhibitions.

Outside Place des Arts, what you'll see depends entirely on when you visit. The above-ground plazas and adjacent small green spaces might be busy with commuters; or it could be rather subdued and abandoned early on a Sunday morning; or every available space – roadways, streets, plazas, adjacent vacant lots and even indoor plazas – might be taken up with stages erected for the **jazz festival**, the **Nuits d'Afrique festival**, the **Francofolies**, or even the mid-winter **Festival Montréal en Lumière** (Montreal High Lights Festival). For such events – and they occur rather regularly in festival-mad Montreal – traffic is diverted and the citizenry and visitors take over the streets.

Modern Developments

Directly south of Place des Arts, across Sainte-Catherine, is **Complexe Desjardins★** (BCY), another mini-city, this one including not just

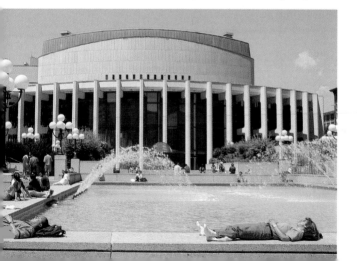

shops and cinemas but offices of the provincial government (which indirectly owns the site) and the Wyndham Hotel. The central plaza is vast enough to serve as a concert and performance venue, either on its own, or in conjunction with one of the many city festivals.

Southward again, across Boulevard René-Lévesque and connected by under-street walkways, is **Complexe Guy-Favreau** (CY), a red-brick-clad warren of federal government offices, shops and apartments. In the continuing Canadian rivalry, Complexe Guy-Favreau loses out to Complexe Desjardins in terms of visual appeal and interest. There is an attractive interior **garden** with benches, however – more sedate than any corner of the provincial counterpart – and the mall provides a sheltered access route to sites to the south.

The march of redevelopment continues with the **Palais des Congrès** (Convention Center), straddling the Ville-Marie Expressway and touching down on one side of a plaza facing Rue de la Gauchetière. As many as 10 000 delegates to conventions and trade shows can be accommodated in dozens of combinable halls – and more, as the center is expanded in the next few years.

Chinatown★

Leading eastward from the Convention Center plaza, La Gauchetière is a pedestrian mall which forms the main thoroughfare of **Chinatown★** (CY). Here you'll find many of the features common to downtown Chinese communities in North America: a traditional gateway (on Boulevard St-Laurent); stores selling bargain-priced shoes, silks and ceramics; groceries filled with exotic foods; and herbal centers. But Montreal's Chinatown also features a number of restaurants that are exceptionally inexpensive, especially at lunch time (just look at the menus posted along La Gauchetière and the even cheaper ones along Clark). You'll see that the signage is stubbornly trilingual (Cantonese, French, English), despite prevailing regulations.

Notable local Chinatown landmarks include the first Chinese laundry, at the corner of St-Antoine and Jeanne-Mance. The Catholic mission at 205 La Gauchetière holds an unusual Oriental-style depiction of the Stations of the Cross.

Eastward from Place des Arts, Rue Sainte-Catherine turns into Montreal's **tenderloin district**, where sex shops are present, if not prominent, and streetwalkers ply their trade. This is also the area where you'll sometimes come across 'squeegee kids', inflicting unwanted windshield cleaning. The scene is rather subdued compared with that in other cities. The **central bus terminal** is just to the east, at the corner of Berri and De Maisonneuve.

No prizes for guessing when you're entering Chinatown!

Latin Quarter

Boulevard St-Laurent was the traditional line
between English and French in Montreal, and
though the whole city is French to varying
degrees today, you'll reach the soul of Montreal
– or Montréal – east of the divide at **Rue St-
Denis★**. The St-Denis area is the center of
Canadian French-language culture, where the
original Université de Montréal, the National
Library of Quebec and live theater flourished.
It became known as the **Latin Quarter** when
several educational institutions were founded
here in the early 20C. The institutions have
changed, but the vocation of the
neighborhood continues. Ranged on both
sides of the narrow, humming thoroughfare
above Sainte-Catherine, and spilling into side
streets and laneways, are cafés, restaurants,
terrasses, bookstores, boutiques, cinemas and
theaters (*see map* p.71).

*Paris meets
L'Amérique du Nord
on Rue St-Denis and
the alleys and lanes
nearby, as music and
conversation spill out
of cafés to outside
tables.*

The **Université de Québec à Montréal** (UQAM) has premises in buildings along the east side of St-Denis below Sainte-Catherine, some of them integrated into the preserved façades of demolished heritage buildings, including the former St James Church which boasts the largest spire in Montreal, at 98m (321ft). The **Théâtre St-Denis** (T), just above De Maisonneuve, is one of the larger general-purpose halls, and has hosted long runs by such contemporary artists as mimic André Philippe Gagnon and chanteuse Céline Dion (before mega-stardom).

Farther up the street, the **Bibliothèque Nationale de Québec** (National Library of Quebec), at no 1700, is an elaborate Beaux-Arts building with antique furnishings and fittings, which attempts to collect every book published in Quebec. The building will see other uses once the library relocates to expanded premises opposite the bus station.

The **Cinémathèque Québecoise** (A), 335 De Maisonneuve East, screens classic and art movies most evenings except Mondays, and is a storehouse of recorded images. Its counterpart just down the street is the **Office National du Film** (National Film Board) (N), at the corner of St-Denis and De Maisonneuve, in modern premises that rise from a traditional townhouse façade. The two institutions often cooperate in presentations of film series. The National Film Board also has an extensive library of films on video disc, where children (and grown-ups) sit in armchairs at control consoles, touch their selections on the screen, and a robot takes care of the rest, jukebox-style.

The traditional bohemian and avant-garde life of St-Denis has migrated northward in recent years, across Sherbrooke to the blocks around Duluth and Rachel, into Plateau Mont-Royal (see p.67). Here are found the boutiques of up-and-coming Quebec designers, as well as more recognized marques.

Join the crowds of tourists and Montrealers and stroll up and down St-Denis, or rest your feet as you sip an apéritif or café au lait. *Le St Malo*, at no 1605, is a long-established eatery popular with students; *Le Commensal*, at no 2115, is part of a successful gourmet vegetarian chain. Farther north, along Rue Duluth to the east of St-Denis, are numerous fine, small and low-priced restaurants, most allowing you to bring your own wine. Among them are *Lombardy*, 411 Duluth East, serving North Italian fare, and *Mi Tierra*, 900 Duluth East, a find for seekers of traditional Mexican (not 'California-style') cuisine. The tab in either of these is usually well under $20.

Carré St-Louis★

A block north of Rue Sherbrooke along St-Denis, on the west side, you'll come to the most genteel of Montreal's city squares, sedate **Carré St-Louis★** (St Louis Square), bordered by 19C and early 20C greystone townhouses, with front gardens (*see map* p.71).

Westward, the pedestrian street leading away from the square is **Rue Prince-Arthur**, lined with Greek, Vietnamese, Polish and Italian restaurants, as well as grocery stores serving the resident population of Portuguese immigrants. The shops are popular with price-conscious students and others on a budget. In warmer weather, when tables are set outside, Prince-Arthur is as fine a locale as any in the city for observing the more offbeat of Montreal's residents and for enjoying the street entertainers, musicians and artists who appear when the sun shines.

Many of the restaurants on Prince-Arthur are not licensed to serve alcohol. Instead, you're invited to bring your own wine (*apportez votre vin* reads the sign in the window). Pick up a bottle at a grocery store, and head inside for your big meal of the day. If you can't decide which to choose, *La Cabane Grecque* will serve a lunch both astonishingly large and low-priced.

Boulevard St-Laurent (The Main)

Continue west to **Boulevard St-Laurent**, known as St Lawrence Boulevard or simply **The Main** (as in Main Street) to English-speakers, where successive immigrant groups originally set up house in Montreal. This lively and colourful ethnic meltingpot has always been one of Montreal's important thoroughfares and is the starting point for streets' east-west numbering. The venerable *Levine's Bakery* on The Main is currently a Portuguese establishment, while the *St-Viateur Bagel Factory*, some blocks north, is under Italian ownership. Each community has its landmarks along The Main, ranging from *Schwartz's Deli* (no 3895) with its incomparable Montreal-style smoked-meat sandwiches on rye bread, to the *Librería Española*, with groceries and newspapers from around Latin America.

The area to the west of St-Laurent, crowded with older houses and a few high rises, is known as the **McGill Ghetto**, after the university that lurks beyond. Northward are the districts known as **Mile End** and **Plateau Mont-Royal★**.

South of Sherbrooke at 2111 St-Laurent is the **Musée Juste pour Rire** (Just for Laughs Museum), unique and somewhat controversial in its attempt to document just what humor is

Characterful townhouses with front gardens open onto the genteel Carré St-Louis.

and how it has developed. (☎ **514 845 4000** to check current opening hours.)

Relatively low rents and property prices, convenience to downtown and universities, and variety in surroundings have led to Soho-style development along The Main. Coexisting with immigrant establishments are trendy cafés, bars, and mini-cinemas. The largest of the new enterprises is **Ex-Centris**, a cinema and arts complex that occupies much of the block on the west side of St-Laurent south of Prince-Arthur. Built in, around, and over existing buildings, it contains several screening rooms for non-Hollywood-style films, as well as a sleek upstairs bar. Even if you're not planning to attend a movie (some subtitled in French with dialogue in English), go in anyway and approach the ticket window, where you'll view the attendant on a screen and lose your sense of who is exactly where.

Street paintings brighten the scene in a street festival, Plateau Mont-Royal.

MORE DOWNTOWN SITES

Gay Village

East from St-Denis, Sainte-Catherine continues past the set of commercial buildings that used to anchor the 'French' downtown, when shops in the central area were considered by many to be 'English' and somewhat alien. As barriers between the communities have broken down, business in the area has declined.

Beyond Rue St-Hubert, the lively bars and cafés are the main thoroughfare of Montreal's large **Village** (short for either 'Village Gaie' or 'Gay Village', near metro Beaudry) (*see map* p.71). Streets are especially narrow in this part of town, but, with low building heights, anything but claustrophobic. Many houses have been carefully spruced up by singles and same-sex couples, with individual touches such as flower boxes and gardens in small streetside plots.

The **St Pierre Apôtre Church** (R) at René-Lévesque and Visitation, a Gothic structure dating from 1851, has the only known chapel dedicated to AIDS victims.

If you come out this way, the **Écomusée du Fier Monde** (2050 Amherst) (M¹), formerly a public bath, memorializes Montreal's industrialization and later de-industrialization, along with life in a working-class district, as this once was. Neighborhood walking tours are given on Sundays in summer (☎ **528 8444** for details; *closed Mon and Tues*).

Atwater Market

Of several public markets in the city, one of the more accessible and varied is Atwater Market, at the corner of Atwater Avenue and the Lachine Canal (*metro:* Lionel Groulx). The clean Art Deco lines of the tan tower are something of a landmark. Browse the stalls and shops (sheltered in winter) for fruits, spices,

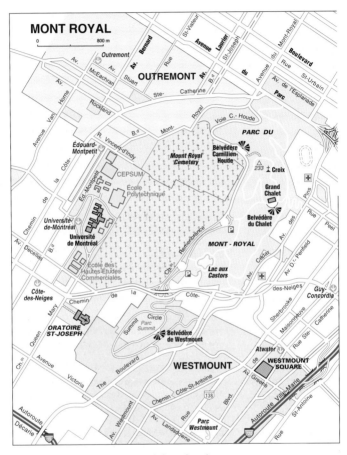

MONT ROYAL

0   800 m

Outremont

Av. McEachran
Rue Stuart

OUTREMONT Av. d

Ste- Catherine

Avenue Van Home

Av. Rockland

Mont- Royal

Voie C.- Houde

PARC DU

Édouard-
Montpetit

R. Vincent-d'Indy

**Mount Royal
Cemetery**

**Belvédère
Camillien-
Houde**

CEPSUM

233 ⊥ Croix

École
Polytechnique

**Grand
Chalet**

Université-
de-Montréal

**Belvédère
du Chalet**

Université
de Montréal

MONT - ROYAL

Av. des Pins

Rue Peel

École des
Hautes Études
Commerciales

Lac aux
Castors

Av. D.- Penfield

Côte-
des-Neiges

Chemin de la

Côte-

des-Neiges

**Guy-
Concordia**

Sherbrooke

Circle
Parc
Summit

**ORATOIRE
ST-JOSEPH**

Summit

**Belvédère
de Westmount**

Maisonneuve

Catherine

Atwater

**WESTMOUNT
SQUARE**

Queen
Avenue

Boulevard

WESTMOUNT

Victoria

The

Chemin Côte-St-Antoine

138 Blvd.

Autoroute
Décarie

Av. Landsdowne

**Parc
Westmount**

Autoroute

St-Antoine

deer and bison sausages, French bread and
cheese, or enjoy a chocolatine and coffee
upstairs. In fine weather, assemble the
ingredients for a picnic. Or cross the pedestrian-
and-cyclist bridge to raise a glass at *Magnan*, a
working man's pub and lobster house.

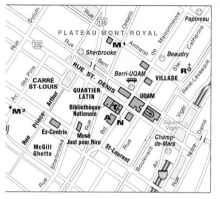

Key

A Cinémathèque québécoise

M¹ Écomusée du Fier Monde

M² Musée des Hospitalières de l'Hôtel-Dieu de Montréal

N Office National du Film

R St Pierre Apôtre Church

T Théâtre St-Denis

MOUNT ROYAL AND SURROUNDING AREAS

Westmount

The western part of Montreal is more English (as in English Canadian) than the rest of the city, and nowhere more so than in Westmount, a separate municipality surrounded by the greater city. To catch the flavor, head toward Greene Avenue (*metro:* Atwater, then walk west along De Maisonneuve Boulevard, or take the underground passageway).

Towering above Greene Avenue (and, of course, also extending downward into a shopping complex) is **Westmount Square★**. Designed by Ludwig Mies van der Rohe, the ensemble is one of the landmarks of modern architecture, revealing its innermost structure through dark structural ribs.

More interesting are the establishments along the avenue: bookstores (*Nicholas Hoare, the Double Hook*), cafés and restaurants (*Bistro on the Avenue, Michael D's*), and shops (*Oink Oink* is the premier toy store on the island, though far from the largest).

Not everyone in the shops *is* English but everybody speaks English. Mercedes and Lexus automobiles vie for the limited parking spaces or simply sit double-parked, as if tickets were not a problem.

Look northward, and you'll see where some of the clients live, in large houses and mansions set upon curving streets and drives ascending **Westmount Mountain**, an extension of Mount Royal. On a nice day, you can walk up to the **Westmount Belvedere** for **views★** of the leafy municipality and out over the St Lawrence River. Or take a taxi up. Less strenuously, continue west along De Maisonneuve to **Westmount Park**, with its English-style paths, heritage library and signature greenhouse (*open all year*).

For more Westmount atmosphere, continue west on Sherbrooke to the main shopping area, around Victoria Avenue. Bus no 24 eastbound will take you back to the center of the city.

Boules in the park, Mount Royal.

Outremont

On the opposite side of Mount Royal, the francophone counterpart of Greene Avenue is **Laurier Avenue**, in the largely French-speaking Outremont (walk west from *metro:* Laurier), also a separate municipality.

Bistros are more avant garde than in Westmount, and pâtisseries, clothing boutiques, cheese shops, fine restaurants (*La Chronique* is currently popular) and sidewalk cafés are more predominant. Four blocks to the north, **Bernard Avenue**, west of Clark, is, if anything, more lively and trendy. *Le Bilboquet*, 1311 Bernard West, has the best ice cream on the island. *Café Souvenir* (no 1261) is popular for brunch on weekends, and there are numerous croissanteries and ethnic restaurants.

After lunch or a snack, take a short stroll

westward to the residential quarter.
Outremont's mansions don't scale the heights,
but they reach onto the lower slopes of Mount
Royal, along Chemin Côte Sainte-Catherine.

Eastward, back toward the metro stations
(either Laurier or Rosemont), Outremont
shows its working-class and cosmopolitan side.
Some of the older multi-family buildings are of
a kind unique to Montreal, with winding and
dangerous outside metal stairways that
conserve interior space (and are no longer
allowed in new construction).

There is a significant population of Hasidic
Jews. Outremont blends into the traditional
immigrant quarters of Plateau Mont Royal. A
must-stop, for Montrealers of any background,
is the *St-Viateur Bagel Shop*, 158 St-Viateur West.

Parc du Mont-Royal★★
(Mount Royal Park)

Mount Royal is the physical heart of Montreal, looming if not towering over the city, and forms its spiritual heart and soul as well. The skeletal metal **cross** atop the mountain beams at night, less as a religious symbol these days than as a link with the past and the first cross planted by French sailors. When the ice storm of 1998 devastated the forests of the mountain, a shudder of dismay and despair passed through many, followed by relief as the trees quickly recovered over the following summers.

Parc du Mont-Royal★★ (Mount Royal Park) is a pioneer city park and oasis, a generous section of countryside in the city, designed by Frederick Law Olmsted (known for Central Park in New York City), and opened in 1876.

Pedestrians may approach from downtown by following Rue Peel up to a steep path. More easily, take bus no 11 from Mont Royal metro station to

scale the mountain along Voie Camillien-Houde and Chemin Remembrance. A good place to start a park exploration is **Lac aux Castors** (Beaver Lake), frequented by boaters in summer. Continue across the meadow, and upward toward the forested area. Paths and trails, from easy to moderate, penetrate the woods.

The focal point of the park is the stone **Grand Chalet**, opening to a belvedere with a magnificent **panorama★★★** of central Montreal below and the lowlands of the St Lawrence River in the distance – a strategic vista in pre-European days, as well as today. Stretching along the northern slopes of the mountain are the vast **Mount Royal Cemetery**, and the **Université de Montréal**, with its signature Art Deco tower designed by Ernest Cormier. Westward along the road through the park is the **Belvédère Camillien-Houde**, most accessible by car, offering

Take in the spectacular view from the mountain that tells the story of Montreal – the Cross of the French settlers, a river into the continent, railroads, fertile lowlands and skyscrapers.

The cross shines out at night.

views★★ to the Olympic Tower and the eastern part of the city.

As busy as it is in summer, Mount Royal Park is most *Montréalais* in the depths of winter. Skaters glide on frozen Beaver Lake between breaks for hot chocolate at the adjacent snack bar. The ski tow starts running, and kids plunge down the hills on sleds. Die-hard joggers and mountain bikers roll and squish through the snow – the colder the temperature, the better. And on trails up to the cross and around the flanks of the mountain swish cross-country skiers, nearly silent in the winter wood.

Oratoire Saint-Joseph★★
(St Joseph's Oratory)

The traditional guiding role of the Catholic church is evident everywhere in Montreal, in surviving churches from the French régime, in convent-school complexes both active and converted to remarkable junior colleges and condominium apartments, in orphanages abandoned as a population strayed from holy dictum and became less reproductive. But nowhere is the faith itself more powerfully evident than at the **Oratoire Saint-Joseph★★** (St Joseph's Oratory, 3800 Chemin Queen Mary, *metro:* Côte des Neiges, or walk from

The massive Oratoire Saint-Joseph's origins go back to the simple chapel of the miracle healer, Brother André.

Mount Royal Park; *open daily*). The oratory was founded by Brother André, to whom miraculous cures were attributed – as indicated by the numerous crutches displayed in the entrance way, which is reached after a climb up steps and across terraces from the street below. The Romanesque-style **Basilica★**, topped by the great dome completed in 1955, reaches high enough (112m/367ft) above neighboring Westmount to be visible from all sides as one approaches Montreal. Inside, the Basilica is surprisingly austere, yet imposing for its massive size. The 56-bell carillon (originally cast for the Eiffel Tower but never used there) provides free recitals. There is a small **museum** dedicated to Brother André.

From the metro station, Chemin de la Côte des Neiges leads northward, and downhill, through a varied neighborhood with Hindu sari shops, numerous Vietnamese restaurants, and a population drawn from the world over. Southward, the wide boulevard runs up and alongside Mount Royal Park to downtown.

ISLANDS IN THE RIVER

Montreal's green space extends right into the St Lawrence River as **Parc Jean Drapeau** (formerly Parc des Îles), largely the legacy of Expo 67, the world fair held on **Île Ste-Hélène★** (St Helen's Island) and man-made **Île Notre-Dame★** (Notre Dame Island). Parc Jean Drapeau is vast, varied and only one subway stop from downtown (*metro:* Île-Ste-Hélène). Bus no 167 from the station makes a loop to include all the island sites. A ferry operates from the Old Port in the summer. By car or on bicycle or inline skates, take the Pont de la Concorde to most sites (parking fee, except at Casino); the eastern part of St Helen's Island is accessible from the Jacques-Cartier Bridge.

Île Ste-Hélène★
(St Helen's Island)

St Helen's Island, closer to the city, has groves of trees, meadows and ageing fortifications, as well as notable sculptures, including *Man*, by Alexander Calder.

The former United States pavilion, the geodesic dome designed by Buckminster Fuller, now functions as the **Biosphere★**, providing a see-through view to the St Lawrence, and an in-depth interpretation of the environment, with an emphasis on undersea life and water resources, through interactive exhibitions and multimedia shows (*open daily in summer, closed Mon rest of year*).

Below: The Biosphere, on Île Ste-Hélène.

*Left: The sculpture
Man stands guard
on the north of the
island.*

The **Vieux-Fort** (Old Fort), a remnant of the
days when Montreal needed protection from
possible American attack, is the only surviving
defensive installation in Montreal. It houses the
David M Stewart Museum★. Exhibits are both
static (artifacts used by French and English
settlers) and dynamic (soldiers and sailors of
re-created French and British regiments, on
maneuver once again) (*open daily May-Sept,
closed Tues rest of year*).

La Ronde, at the downriver end of St Helen's
Island, is Montreal's large summer amusement
park (*see* p.109).

Île Notre-Dame★
(Notre Dame Island)

*The Old Fort, built
by the British in the
1820s as defence
against possible
American attack.*

Notre Dame Island was expanded from an
embankment along the St Lawrence Seaway
with infill, largely from excavations for
Montreal's metro. Its principal attraction is the

Casino, housed in the former French pavilion of the world fair (*see* p.109 for details).

The island is perfect for late-spring-to-early-fall strolling, cycling and inline skating. Among the sites on offer are the **Jardins des Floralies**, a floral park with exotic decorative plantings; the Grand Prix **Gilles-Villeneuve** racetrack; and a lake and beach, popular in the summer. Entrance is free, except to the beach and for rowboat hire.

As fascinating as anything on the island are the operations of the adjacent **St Lawrence Seaway**, along which ocean-going ships lumber, their upper decks appearing from a distance to be land-bound prairie schooners. For a closer look, walk over to the Victoria Bridge at the upriver end of the island, sections of which are raised to allow passage. The nearby **St Lambert Lock★** may be seen at closer range from a point accessible by road on the south bank of the river.

Tempt Lady Luck at the Casino, on Île Notre-Dame.

Habitat 67, a futuristic complex of apartments, is one of the architectural legacies of Expo 67.

Snack stands abound, but consideration should be given to some of the more formal dining establishments on the island. The Casino has a moderately priced Italian restaurant, and *Nuances*, one of the finest establishments in the entire city (*see* p.99). *Le Festin du Gouverneur*, in the Old Fort, and the *Hélène de Champlain* recreate the atmosphere of the French régime.

Cité du Havre

Cité du Havre is a set of buildings along the embankment that encloses the port of Montreal, on the way to Parc Jean Drapeau. Most notable, and still unique, is **Habitat 67★**, Moshe Safdie's set of prefabricated apartment units apparently dropped into place at odd angles like so many children's blocks, each affording privacy and air space in the same way as single-family houses.

PARC OLYMPIQUE★★
(OLYMPIC PARK)

Montreal breaks with urban tradition, in that its signature structure is not downtown, but in the working-class East End of the city. The leaning **Olympic Tower** once supported a retractable roof on the adjacent **Stade Olympium** (Olympic Stadium), built for the 1976 games. The engineering never quite worked, but the tower is a landmark nevertheless, with a cable-car ride available to take in the sweeping **view**★★★ from the top, unhindered by any nearby large structures. (*metro:* Pie-IX or Viau, cable-car departures every 10 minutes, admission charge.)

The stadium is Montreal's Colosseum, where cheers and jeers are magnified as they echo off the now-permanent roof. Montreal Expos baseball games are announced in French, of

The Olympic Stadium and the famous leaning tower, which affords views stretching over 80km on a clear day.

course, as well as in English, an unusual experience for any fan. The adjacent **Olympic Pool** is open to the public when not in use for competition. A couple of guided tours of the entire complex are available daily in either English or French.

Nearby, the **Biodôme**★ is a step beyond zoo and botanical garden. Originally built for the Olympic cycling events, the distinctive **building**★ now houses an imaginative museum of environmental and natural sciences, with four climatic zones, including the Polar north, the St Lawrence River, the Canadian forest and the tropics, each at the appropriate temperature, complete with living fauna and flora (*open daily*).

The horticultural exuberance of the Jardin Botanique will lift the spirits and soothe the soul.

Northward across Rue Sherbrooke, Montreal's **Jardin Botanique**★★ (Botanical Garden), in **Maisonneuve Park**, is the second-largest in the world, with 26 000 species in the

open and in ten **conservatories★**.
Musts include the Japanese
Garden and Pavilion, the
Chinese Garden★, and the Tree
House, with its collection of
bonsais.

The adjacent **Insectarium★**,
built in the shape of a giant
insect, offers insights into the
world of butterflies and bugs,
with an extensive collection of
preserved and live species, and
even, occasionally, tastings of
insects as prepared in other cultures (*open
daily*). A free shuttle service operates between
the park, Botanical Gardens and Biodôme.

*The Insectarium has
an extensive exhibits
of preserved
specimens – and
some live ones too!*

One other nearby site, the **Château
Dufresne★**, a fine merchant mansion a block
west of the junction of Pie-IX and Sherbrooke,
houses a collection of furniture and decorative
items.

MORE NEIGHBORHOODS AND NEARBY TOWNS

Pick up a metro map and choose from any of
the neighborhoods of Montreal that suit your
interest.

The De l'Eglise station is on Rue Wellington,
in the heart of **Verdun** in south-western
Montreal, a charming and thoroughly mixed
English-French working-class district with
dozens of mom-and-pop stores where bargains
are to be found. Just a block to the south, a
park faces the St Lawrence River and **Île des
Sœurs** (Nuns' Island), an enclave of
condominium development.

Four stations further on is Angrignon
station, at **Parc Angrignon**, site of a farm open
to visitors (reserve farm visits by calling ☎ **514
872 2816**, summer only).

Pointe St-Charles – 'The Point' – is a working-class area that once housed Irish immigrants who worked on the construction of the Victoria Bridge. Somewhat run-down these days, bordered by rail yards and industry, it includes the landmark **Maison St-Gabriel★** (2146 Place Dublin, *metro:* Square Victoria, bus no 61), one of the oldest houses on the island. Dating from about 1698, with characteristically steep roof and stone construction, it sheltered the *filles du roy*, orphan girls who were sent to Nouvelle France to find husbands and populate the colony. Period furnishings and artifacts are on display.

Parc Avenue, running north from Sherbrooke near Place des Arts, is the axis of Montreal's **Greek** community.

Of several **Italian** areas, the largest is along Jean Talon Boulevard, in the vicinity of the metro stop of the same name. The **Jean Talon Market**, a few blocks to the west, is worth a visit.

Lachine

Lachine, at the western end of the canal, is a waterfront suburb with a number of venerable buildings that date from the days of the fur trade. Take bus no 110 from Angrignon metro station, or cycle along the Lachine Canal, to reach the riverside sculpture park, a fun stroll on any summer day. The harbor shelters recreational watercraft in summer.

The **Fur Trade in Lachine National Historic Site** in a period depot on waterfront St-Joseph Boulevard at 12th Ave in Lachine, tells the story of the commerce on which Montreal was built, through an interactive exhibition. The canal itself is explained at the adjacent **Lachine Canal Interpretation Center** (*open in summer, closed Mon am*). The **Lachine Museum**, on LaSalle Boulevard, is a charming collection of artifacts of local history and toy trains.

The Western Suburbs

For a tour of the leafy **western suburbs** of Montreal, take the no 211 bus from metro Lionel Groulx all the way to **Ste-Anne-de-Bellevue★** (almost 30km/18.5 miles and an hour away, all on one metro ticket, but avoid rush hours). Ste-Anne is a charming waterside village, with cafés overlooking a marina and locks that connect Lake St-Louis, a wide spot in the St Lawrence, with Lake of Two Mountains, at the mouth of the Ottawa River.

Nearby sites, best visited by automobile or taxi, include the **Macdonald Campus Farm** of McGill University, Lakeshore Road; **Morgan Arboretum**, Chemin Ste-Marie at Pine, with walking paths and cross-country ski trails; and the **Ecomuseum**, 21125 Chemin Ste-Marie, which houses live animals of the St Lawrence valley.

EXCURSIONS

An outing from Montreal to a nearby ski center, town, or park, will usually require your own car or a rental vehicle.

Kahnawake

The historic Mohawk Native American ('Indian') community of Kahnawake (or Caughnawaga) lies just across the St Lawrence from the western suburbs of Montreal. Stubbornly independent, Kahnawake has its own peace force and treaty rights that transcend national borders – sometimes to the irritation of various taxing authorities.

Visitors are welcome to arrange a walking or driving tour (contact Kahnawake Tourism Office, ☎ **450 638 9699**), to include the shrine of Blessed Kateri Tekakwitha (beatified in 1980), the historic **church** and the Mohawk cultural center. Buses from Montreal run eight

Mont St-Sauveur, in the Laurentian Mountains – less than an hour from Montreal!

times daily (call the tourism office for details), or drive.

Laurentian Mountains★★

The closest ski resorts, **Mont St-Sauveur** and **Ste-Adèle**, are just 60km (37 miles) north of Montreal along Autoroute 15. St-Sauveur is the oldest Laurentian resort, and is now one of the largest, with an attractive, lively village; it also operates water slides during the warm weather.

The most distant ski area in this direction, and also the largest, is **Mont Tremblant**, about 120km (75 miles) away. Tremblant is a lively resort, set on the shores of the lake, and its beauty and year-round attractions make it very popular. Its activities are more comprehensive than some of the other resorts, and include watersports and snowshoeing (*see* p.110).

Montrealers have traditionally flocked to the

cool Laurentians in summer.
Activities include country drives
through the picturesque towns
of the area, including **Ste-Adèle**
and **Ste-Agathe★**, and **Ste-
Marguerite★** on Lake Masson,
with stops for antique- and craft-
shopping, and country dining. A
scenic loop road, open in
summer, leads through **Mont
Tremblant Park★**, then curves
eastward and southward back
down to Ste-Agathe. A 200km (125 miles)
linear park, suitable for cycling, runs from St-
Jérôme, 50km (31 miles) north of Montreal,
along a former railroad right of way.

*Snowmobiling in the
Laurentides.*

Eastern Townships★★

The Townships, east of Montreal, were settled
by Loyalist refugees from the newly
independent United States, so many place
names are English. Set in the mountainous
region of the Appalachians, it is a region of
wooded hills, steep valleys and picturesque
lakes. Stay in one of the many B&Bs or on a
farm B&B and discover the local wineries and
ostrich farms.

Ski areas include **Mont-Sutton**, **Mont-Orford**

*In summer, the
Laurentides provide
a tranquil and scenic
escape from the city.*

and **Mont Owl's-Head**. Also popular is **Jay Peak**, across the border in Vermont. **Lake Memphremagog** is a popular summer destination, mostly for owners of summer cottages, though there are motels and inns in **Magog★**, **North Hatley★** and **Ste-Catherine-de-Hatley**. At the eastern limit of the townships, just south of the city of **Sherbrooke★**, picturesque **Lennoxville** is still largely English-speaking, home to the small Bishop's University. To the west, closer to Montreal, is the charming village of **Knowlton★**, on Lake Brome. Almost any drive along the byways takes one through hilly terrain, around curves revealing lakes and woods and maple bush.

With or without children, summer driving trips to the Townships can be combined with a visit to the **Granby Zoo★** (Exit 68, Autoroute 10, 80km/50 miles south-east of Montreal) or **Parc Safari** (near Hemmingford, Exit 6, Autoroute 15). Drive through the park in your car to see the animals that roam freely. There are also beaches, picnic area and an amuseument park, making it an excellent attraction for children.

The Benedictine abbey at Saint-Benoît-du-Lac overlooks the serene Lake Memphremagog.

THE SPIRIT OF MONTREAL

Montreal is a late-night jazz session under the stars on the terrace of Place des Arts, free to all comers … an incomparable nouvelle cuisine meal at a surprisingly low price … ice skating on the St Lawrence River or whooshing silently on cross-country skis on Mount Royal in the dead of winter… the thrill and anticipation of playing the slots at the Casino … people-watching from a sidewalk café on Rue St-Denis. Montrealers weave enjoyment into work, business and every aspect of life. Best of all, they welcome you to take part in the fun.

Montreal is about the conquest of climate, both in solid, snug constructions and in spirit.

Where else are winter celebrations – La Fête des Neiges and the High Lights Festival – as much a part of the tourist calendar as summer attractions? Where else are thoughts of winter swept away as flowers take over not just private gardens but public spaces at the first signs of spring?

Montreal is the aroma of all the cultures that are still creating the city – croissants and *café chaud*, a baguette with cheese, bagels cooked in a wood-burning oven, *souvlaki* on pita, *tourtière* and beans with maple syrup, smoked meat on rye enjoyed by people of all backgrounds.

Montreal is the French-speaker with the Irish name, the English-rights activist with the French name, and the masses of people with assorted backgrounds who

Montreal in winter.

manage to get-along-very-well-thank-you despite the political storms that occasionally blow through.

It's the city of struggle in a French world depicted in Gabrielle Roy's *Bonheur d'occasion* (*The Tin Flute*), and the city of getting ahead in English and Yiddish in Mordecai Richler's *The Apprenticeship of Duddy Kravitz*, and English and French as partners and strangers in Hugh MacLennan's *Two Solitudes*.

Montreal is a celebration of people, seasons, good taste, *le bon accueil*, all distinct and yet together, and there to enjoy.

WEATHER

Montreal's climate can run to extremes in *both* winter and summer, but bouts of hot, humid weather or sub-arctic chill usually blow out as predictably as they arrive. Conventional visitors, of course, will time their arrivals to take advantage of mild weather in late spring, summer, and early fall. But those who wish to get into the spirit of Montreal will appreciate life in a city tuned to all seasons, and take advantage of lower winter accommodation rates as well.

The average high temperature in July is just under 26°C (80°F), while night-time lows average just over 16°C (60°F). The weather is usually predictable, with short, moderate rains and occasional thunderstorms, but the tail ends of hurricanes can sometimes blow up from the Atlantic and drench the city. Hot spells that affect the United States are felt with less intensity, but most houses have air conditioners, and use them.

Temperatures cool off into autumn at varying rates from year to year. 1 October is usually considered the last reliable frost-free night. With any luck, an Indian summer will provide pleasant and crisp strolling weather well into November. By mid-November, nights are usually below freezing.

By December, winter has arrived, with intermittent heavy snows and temperatures that occasionally plunge to night-time lows of −30°C (−22°F) as the jet stream moves south and polar air sweeps in. But frozen conditions usually move on quickly. The average high in January is a more moderate −6°C (21°F), the low −15°C (5°F). Montrealers often speak of the 'January thaw', but it may come in December, or February, or both. Temperatures will stay consistently above freezing, snow will melt, and there could even be spells of rain.

Though Montreal is one of the snowiest large cities in the world, snow is usually removed efficiently from both streets and sidewalks. Brigades of blowers, scrapers, and pint-sized sidewalk ploughs are one of the more offbeat tourist sights.

Visitors should be prepared for the extremes of winter. Warm clothing and boots are musts – many items can be purchased locally. The usual etiquette is to carry a pair of slip-on shoes to be worn inside.

By mid-March, there are mild days, and blustery ones, and sometimes a day that is both, when some residents will still be wearing boots while others will be in sandals. An occasional wet, heavy snow can fall into April, but average highs for the month are about 52°F (11°C). Soon, bicycle racks are placed on city sidewalks, flowers are set in planters throughout the city, and winter fades into memory. By 1 June, nights are frost-free, and daylight lasts until almost 9pm.

CALENDAR OF EVENTS

Montreal is a city of festivals: musical celebrations, cinema, food, light, language, gender preference, racing cars, religion and much more. The larger events, such as the Jazz Festival, take over streets, parks, and public and private venues.

Fête des Neiges (Winter Carnival), January-February on St Helen's Island, celebrates winter with ice sculptures, snow slides, skating, and more.

Festival Montréal en Lumière (Montreal High Lights Festival), in February, newest of the annual celebrations, is a tripartite celebration of culinary arts, music, and, most unusually, public illumination.

Festival de Théâtre des Amériques (Theater Festival of the Americas), May-June, showcases contemporary drama from around the hemisphere.

Tour de l'Île (Island Circuit), early June, is a one-day amateur bicycle marathon, very popular with Montrealers and visitors.

Chamber Music Festival, mid June, offers concerts atop Mount Royal.

Festival Présence Autochtone (First Peoples' Festival), mid-June, parades and events celebrating the native peoples of the Americas.

Traditional dancing at the First Peoples' Festival.

Grand Prix du Canada, mid June, one of the two Formula I races in North America.

Benson & Hedges International, mid June-late July, spectacular international fireworks competition on St Helen's Island.

Festival International de Jazz de Montréal, early July, the premier jazz gathering, with 300 free concerts.

Festival Juste pour Rire (Just for Laughs Festival), mid July, unofficial humor in both official languages.

Festival Nuits d'Afrique (African Nights), mid July, throbbing rhythms from Africa and the Caribbean.

Diverse Cité, early August, is Montreal's Gay Pride celebration, with art, parades and concerts, centering on the Village area east of downtown.

Les Francofolies, early August, a celebration of French-language comedy and music, with free shows in the Place des Arts area.

Les Fêtes Gourmandes, mid August, is a world food festival on St Helen's Island.

World Film Festival, late August to early September, is a cinemaniacs marathon, offering hundreds of films from all nations.

Festival International de Nouvelle Danse, early October (every two years), celebrates new dance.

Black & Blue Festival, early October, is one of the largest gay celebrations anywhere.

Fireworks light up the city sky.

Festival of New Cinema and New Media, mid October, focuses on documentaries and independent videos.

Coup de Cœur Francophone, early November, celebrates French-language music.

ACCOMMODATIONS

Montreal offers a variety of accommodations in comfortable, safe neighborhoods, ranging from dormitory beds in youth hostels and universities, to tasteful, luxurious lodging at prices that would be hard to match in other countries.

Most **hotels** above the budget and moderate levels price their rooms to some degree according to demand, so rates mentioned

below should be considered representative – you could pay more, or much less. For example, a room at the *Delta* that goes for $340 on a walk-in basis might drop to $150 if booked well in advance, or with a corporate rate or other discount. It's safe to say that lower prices are available on weekends and in winter, and that it's usually not hard to find a room for about $100 (US$70), at most times of the year.
A few local peculiarities:

• Room rates are generally quoted exclusive of taxes, which add another 15 per cent to the price.

• The price for one person is generally the same as, or almost as much as, the price for two, except at budget hotels and bed-and-breakfasts.

• Parking charges at downtown hotels will generally be at least $12 per day.

• Breakfast is not included except at B&Bs, though many hotels have in-room coffee-makers.

Bed-and-breakfasts are rarely devoted entirely to lodging, except for a few upscale establishments. More often in Montreal, they're houses or apartments with one or two spare rooms to let, and are higher up on the price scale, relatively, than B&Bs in England or pensions on the European continent.

Most visitors will probably prefer to stay in the central area (downtown or Old Montreal). An alternative, if you arrive by car, is to stay on the south shore, in Longueuil, and take the metro into town.

It's a good idea, if you're already in North America, to call a toll-free (freephone) number (starting with **800**, **888**, or **877**) to inquire about availability of rooms and prices, or to consult a hotel web site.

Rates quoted by the chains below may be lower or higher than those quoted directly by a hotel.

Comfort Inn ☎ **800 228 5151**
Best Western ☎ **800 528 1234**
Crowne Plaza ☎ **800 227 6963**
Days Inn ☎ **800 329 7466**
Hilton Hotels ☎ **800 445 8667**
Holiday Inn ☎ **800 465 4329**
Marriott ☎ **800 321 2211**
Radisson ☎ **800 333 3333**
Ramada ☎ **800 228 2828**
Sheraton/Westin ☎ **800 228 3000**

The agencies mentioned below handle bookings for all major downtown hotels and might offer rates lower than those available directly from a hotel's reservation office:
Reservation Center of Montreal
☎ **800 567 8687**
Hospitality Canada ☎ **800 665 1258**

Recommendations

Star ratings are provided by the local tourist office. Generally, five-star hotels have indoor pool, extensive shopping, business floors and superior service. Four-star hotels have an indoor pool, several restaurants and fewer shops. Three-star hotels have limited restaurant facilities, but usually have at least a fitness room. Two-star hotels provide no food services. One-star hotels are basic. Rates, in Canadian currency, are for two persons unless otherwise noted.

Five Star

Hilton Montréal Bonaventure (Place Bonaventure H5A 1E4, ☎ 514 878 2332, fax 514 878 3881). Near Central Station, its brusque exterior conceals extensive gardens; heated outdoor pool open in winter. $150-$350.

Hôtel Inter-Continental Montréal (360 Rue St-Antoine Ouest H2Y 3X4, ☎ 514 987 9900, 800 361 3600, fax 514 847 8550). In the World Trade Center, near Old Montreal, with residential-style plush furnishings and intimate public areas; though large, it has the air of a boutique hotel. $155-$375.

Le Centre Sheraton (1201 Boulevard René-Lévesque Ouest H3B 2L7, ☎ 514 878 2000, fax 514 878 3958). Large both in height (37 floors) and number of rooms (825), with especially good meeting facilities, club-like business lounge with superb city views. $200-$330.

Château Champlain (Place du Canada, H3B 4C9, ☎ 514 878 9000, 800 200 5909, fax 514 878 6761). The 'cheese grater' (because of its recessed oval windows) is easy to find, near major business buildings; traditionally furnished. $150-$400.

Hôtel Ritz-Carlton (1228 Rue Sherbrooke Ouest, H3G 1H6, ☎ 514 842 4212, 800 363 0366, fax 514 842 6722). Grande dame of Montreal hostelries; elegant, panelled dining rooms, courtyard with duck pond (but no pool), 229 rooms fitting for any mansion. $170-$500.

Hôtel Vogue (1425 Rue de la Montagne, H3G 1Z3, ☎ 514 285 5555, 800 465 6654, fax 514 849 8903). Plain outside; sumptuous, if cramped, inside. $195-$500.

Four-Star

Courtyard Marriott (410 Rue Sherbrooke Ouest, H3A 1B3, ☎ 514 844 8855, 800 449 6654, fax 514 844 0912). Predictable lodging with indoor pool, near large department stores. $110-$185.

Holiday Inn Montreal Midtown (420 Rue Sherbrooke Ouest, H3A 1B4, ☎ 514 842 6111, 800 387 3042, fax 514 842 9381). Similar to the Courtyard Marriott, and close by, with indoor pool. $115-$185.

Holiday Inn Sélect (99 Rue Viger, H2Z 1E9, ☎ 514 878 9888, 800 878 9888, fax 514 878 6341). In Chinatown and convenient to the

Convention Center, breaks the mould of Holiday Inns with pagoda-topped roofs and Chinese decor and furnishings. $125-$260.

Hôtel de la Montagne (1430 Rue de la Montagne, H3G 1Z5, ☎ 514 288 5656, 800 361 6262, fax 514 288 9658). Moderately sized (135 rooms), in the center of the restaurant and bar scene; rooftop pool. $155-$260.

Hôtel Wyndham (1255 Rue Jeanne-Mance, H5B 1E5, ☎ 514 285 1450, 800 361 8234, fax 514 285 1243). In Place Desjardins, at the heart of the jazz and other festivals; superb facilities.

Novotel (1180 Rue de la Montagne, H3G 1Z1, ☎ 514 861 6000, 800 668 6835, fax 514 861 0992). Outpost of the French chain of streamlined, businesslike hotels. No pool.

Delta Centre-Ville (777 Rue University, H3C 3Z7, ☎ 514 879 1370, fax 514 879 1761). Large, convenient to both downtown and Old Montreal, full facilities (pool, health club, revolving rooftop restaurant). $155-$265.

Three-Star

Travelodge (50 Boulevard René-Lévesque Ouest, H2Z 1A2, ☎ 514 874 9090, 800 578 7878, fax 514 874 0907). Near Chinatown and Place des Arts; no frills, continental breakfast included. $70-$140.

Best Western Europa (1240 Rue Drummond, H3G 1V7, ☎ 514 866 6492, 800 361 3000, fax 514

861 4089). Good value in busy central area. $110-$280.

Best Western Tour Versailles (1808 Rue Sherbrooke Ouest, H3H 1E5, ☎ 514 933 8111, 888 933 8111, fax 514 933 7102). Quieter area at the western end of downtown, with rooms in a modern tower and townhouses. $110-$275.

Hôtel de l'Institut (3535 Rue St-Denis, H2X 3P1, ☎ 514 282 5120, 800 361 5111, fax 514 873 9893). In an office building near the heart of the Latin Quarter; fun, attentive service from hotel-school students. $110-$155.

Le Jardin d'Antoine (2024 Rue St-Denis, H2X 3K7, ☎ 514 843 4506, 800 361 6162, fax 514 281 1481). Boutique hotel in Latin Quarter.

Two-Star

Hôtel Viger (1001 Rue St-Hubert, H2L 3Y3, ☎ 514 845 6058, 800 845 6058, fax 514 844 6068). Near the bus station and Latin Quarter, in a building with character, air-conditioned. $55-$75.

Manoir St-Denis (2006 Rue St-Denis, H2X, ☎ 514 843 3670, 888 467 7654, fax 514 844 2188). Latin Quarter location, with terrace restaurant; good value, breakfast included. $50 single, $60 double.

Hôtel St-Denis (1254 Rue St-Denis, H2X 3J6, ☎ 514 849 4526, 800 363 3364, fax 514 849 4529). Basic-to-decent rooms almost in the heart of the Latin Quarter;

classy old brick building.
$45-$100.

One-Star
Castel St-Denis (2099 Rue St-Denis, H2X 3K8, ☎ 514 842 9719, fax 514 843 8492). Small, friendly economy hotel (18 rooms) in the Latin Quarter. $55-$60.

Bed and Breakfast
Les Passants du San Soucy (171 Rue St-Paul Ouest, H2Y 1Z5, ☎ 514 842 2634, fax 514 842 2912). Heritage stone building in Old Montreal, furnished with antiques and collectibles. $125-$200.

Pierre du Calvet a.d. 1725 (405 Rue Bonsecours, H2Y 3C3, ☎ 514 282 1725, fax 514 282 0456). Restored French-régime town home, furnished with heirlooms. $180-$250.

Bed & Breakfast Networks
These organizations will book individual rooms, in downtown and outlying neighborhoods, from $40 for a single, $50 for a double:

Downtown Network (3458 Ave Laval, H2X 3C8, ☎ 514 289 9749, 800 267 5180).

City-Wide Network (422 Rue Cherrier, H2L 1G9, ☎ 514 738 9410, 800 738 4338).

Dorval Airport
Most hotel chains have locations near the airport.

Hilton Montréal Aéroport
(Dorval H9P 1B7, ☎ 514 631 2411, fax 514 631 0192). In the airport grounds; excellent dining. $140 upwards.

South Shore
Hôtel Radisson Longueuil-Montréal (999 Rue de Sérigny, Longueuil J4K 2T1, ☎ 450 670 3030, 800 493 7303, fax 450 670 5928). Just one block from the metro station for Montreal. $90 upwards for a double (parking included).

Youth Hostels, YMCA and Dorms
Montreal Youth Hostel (1030 Rue Mackay, H3G 2H1, ☎ 514 843 3317, fax 514 934 3251). Low-traffic district, not far from lively western downtown area; dorm beds from $23.

Downtown YMCA (1450 Rue Stanley, H3A 2W6, ☎ 514 849 8393, fax 514 849 7821). Central; singles for men from $45, doubles from $65.

YWCA (1355 Boulevard René-Lévesque Ouest, H3G 1T3, ☎ 514 866 9941, fax 514 866 4866). Singles for women $45, doubles $70, dorm beds $25.

FOOD AND DRINK
Montreal is a culinary meeting place: of *haute cuisine française* and hearty Québecois fare of *tourtière* and *hot-dogs steamés*; plain American and English-Canadian steaks and chops, and new-style

light fare emphasizing fresh local ingredients; fast food American-style, and French-style (*croissants et café*), and kosher-style (bagels and smoked meat sandwiches) and Greek (*souvlaki*); and restaurants offering superb adaptations of the best cuisines from around the world. Best of all, the price for quality food is generally lower than in Europe or the United States.

French and Québecois

The best restaurants unapologetically serve French-style food. Sauces are complex, cheeses fragrant, vegetables crisp. But local sourcing of ingredients such as *cerises de terre* (ground cherries) in season, or venison or bison, lends a Montreal air.

Quebec-style food most often appears in diners on suburban strips, in working-class neighborhoods, and in shopping-center food courts. Generally, it's familiar fare with minor adaptations or trimmings: a crock of beans with maple syrup, *tourtière* (meat pie), a hot dog steamed rather than grilled, roast chicken served with gravy, sugar pie (*tarte au sucre*), or the much-maligned *poutine* (French fries topped with cheddar-cheese curds and gravy).

Canadians dine at a relatively early hour. Service will be available at 6pm, if not earlier, and sometimes there will be a price break for 'early birds.'

French and California wines are generally served with meals, though some of the Niagara-region wines from Ontario are worth trying (ask when ordering). Canadian ice wine is an especially refreshing and unusual after-dinner drink. And beers from local small breweries – McAuslan fruit beers, Boréale, and others – are worth testing, and adopting.

The prices given below cover main course, appetizer or dessert, a drink, tax and a tip. To enjoy excellent food at bargain prices, take your main meal at lunchtime, when most restaurants offer a fixed-price special.

Recommendations
Over $50
Le Passe-Partout (3857 Boulevard Décarie, ☎ **514 487 7750**) Tucked behind a west-end bakery (*metro:* Villa-Maria, or taxi),

The famous St-Viateur Bagel bakery.

sought out by visiting gourmands, creative offerings change daily. Reserve for dinner or lunch; not always open.

Les Halles (1450 Rue Crescent) Longstanding fine French townhouse restaurant, classic and nouvelle cuisine, lunch special.

Nuances (Casino, Île Notre-Dame) Fine wood panelling, leather seating and crystal belie the slot machines outside one of the city's top restaurants. Classic French preparation, using local and exotic foods (smoked duck, soup with lemongrass and coconut).

Toqué! (3842 Rue St-Denis, ☎ 514 499 2084) Sleek and relaxed, this rivals the best of Paris and leaves New York behind. Complex dishes (such as rosemary halibut with vinaigrette of grapefruit) often change; tasting menu. Reserve.

Beaver Club (900 Boulevard René-Lévesque Ouest, Queen Elizabeth Hotel) Just as business in Montreal has turned from English to French, so has the brick-and-beamed club of tycoons, adding fine French fare to traditional roast beef and rack of lamb.

$35-$50

Zen (1050 Rue Sherbrooke Ouest) Incomparable Oriental haute cuisine in sleek *art moderne* setting. Also *prix-fixe* and lunch specials.

Ritz Carlton (1228 Rue Sherbrooke Ouest) Elegant hotel dining; buffet lunch in Café de Paris or around the duck pond.

Chez La Mère Michel (1209 Rue Guy, ☎ 514 934 0473) Long-time favorite for French cuisine in greystone townhouse; specialties include bison tournedos and tarragon lamb knobs; table d'hôte.

La Tour de Ville (Delta Centre-Ville Hotel, 777 Rue University, ☎ 514 879 1370) Montreal's only revolving restaurant with spectacular views. Theme menus. Open evenings, Sunday brunch.

Bleu Marin (1437A Rue Crescent) Fine seafood with subtle Italian touches, on the liveliest street on the west side.

Laloux (250 Avenue des Pins Est) Popular outpost of the Latin Quarter on a somewhat dreary street, bare decor, huge windows, and excellent nouvelle cuisine (from crab ravioli to caribou mignon), and a good choice of cheeses.

Le Parchemin (1333 Rue University) In the old parish house of Christ Church Cathedral; traditional French fare with local touches, including marinated bison; less expensive at lunchtime, including a bargain express menu with a glass of wine included.

Gibby's (298 Place d'Youville) Romantic 18C stone building;

excellent steak and seafood.

$15-$35

Carlos & Pepes (1420 Rue Peel) Ever-lively emporium of California-Mexican food, margaritas and beer.

Le Commensal (1204 McGill College Avenue, 1720 St-Denis and elsewhere) Buffet of innovative vegetarian cuisine at gourmet heights, paid for by weight.

Le Taj (2077 Rue Stanley) Tandoori (clay-pot) cooking is the specialty; the decor is plush. Table d'hôte dinner and inexpensive lunch buffet.

Katsura (2170 Rue de la Montagne) Classic Japanese dining, from sushi to teriyaki steak; easy-choice dinner combinations in soothing surroundings.

Churrascaria Le Milsa (2045 Rue Crescent) A Brazilian-style parade of meats brought to your table, at table d'hôte prices.

Stash (200 Rue St-Paul Ouest) Venerable Polish establishment; generous portions of boar, borsht, stuffed cabbage and brown bread go down well on cold days.

Magnan (2602 Rue St-Patrick, *metro:* Charlevoix) Cavernous workingman's tavern near Atwater Market, welcomes the middle class for lobster, roast beef and cheap beer. (Or try Atwater Market itself, across the Lachine Canal, for superb coffee, croissants, and sandwiches on crusty bread.)

Le Petit Moulinsart (139 Rue St-Paul Ouest) Homage to Tintin, the Belgian comic hero, and his favourite mussels, lamb, fries and beers.

Outdoor dining is the order of the day in summer.

Under $15

La Cabane Grecque (102 Rue Prince-Arthur Est) One of a dozen bring-your-own-wine restaurants on this pedestrian street, offering huge, bargain Greek meals.

Basha (930 Rue Sainte-Catherine Ouest, upstairs) The Lebanese fast food from the counter is good; it's fun to look down to the busy street below, and at your fellow diners.

Bens (990 Boulevard de Maisonneuve Ouest) The downtown deli for the rich, famous and powerful.

Schwartz's (3895 St-Laurent) The worldwide king of the art and science of smoked-meat sandwiches.

La Belle Province (1440 Rue Sainte-Catherine Ouest, many other locations, some labelled **Bellepro**) Wonderful diner decor, Québecois fast food of all origins: *hot-dogs steamés* (steamed), excellent hamburgers, superb if greasy French fries, *pogos* (breaded hot dog on a stick), *poutine* and smoked meat.

Nickels (710 Rue Sainte-Catherine Ouest, other locations) Chanteuse Céline Dion's own chain, brings together smoked meat, roast chicken with gravy, and all the favorites of locals in a retro-rock setting.

Beauty's (93 Avenue Mt-Royal Ouest, *metro:* Mont-Royal) is a retro (or never-updated) diner where omelettes and bagels topped with cream cheese and 'nova' (salmon) are served quickly until 5pm.

Croissant Plus (Place Montréal Trust, McGill College/Sainte-Catherine and elsewhere) Montreal-style fast food, croissants with sandwich fillings.

Café Santropol (3990 Rue St-Urbain) Sixties Plateau Mont-Royal café, huge cheese-fruit-nut sandwiches on slabs of bread, dense soups; storefront premises maintained but never updated.

Underground City:

Les Halles de la Gare (Central Station) Attractive variety of food shops to assemble a meal inexpensively, from **Oktoberfest**'s sausages to the **Boulangerie**'s boxed volaille en croûte to burritos, to be consumed in a trompe l'oeil 'library.' In **Place Ville-Marie** (enter at University and Cathcart), the cheery **Marché Mövenpick** offers salads, crêpes and sandwiches on baguettes. Ethnic snacks are available at other connected concourses: Place Montréal Trust, Eaton Centre, Les Promenades de la Cathédrale.

SHOPPING

Montrealers love to shop, and shopaholic visitors will not be disappointed with the range of goods on offer and the number of shopping areas to explore.

They range from high-fashion outlets featuring products with flair and good taste; through shops specializing in Canadian and Québecois maple candy and crafts; to purveyors of t-shirts and similar tourist trinkets. There are blue jeans and running shoes, or computer peripherals which, because of the devalued Canadian dollar and relatively low wage rates (among industrialized countries) could well be a bargain, depending on where your home is. The choice is yours.

Paying

Credit cards are generally most convenient, and will incur the most favorable exchange rate. Visa and MasterCard are the most widely accepted. Novus (Discover) cards are not recognized in any shops in Canada. Carry Canadian cash for small purchases. US dollars and travelers checks (cheques) are accepted but usually at unfavorable rates.

Taxing Matters

Comparison of prices is a complex matter. Remember to take into account the exchange rate between Canadian dollars and your home currency, and how much tax, if any, would be added to your purchases at home. Visitors should bear in mind that prices shown in Canada almost never include the federal GST (goods-and-services tax, equivalent to VAT) and provincial tax. The total tax bite runs to about 15 per cent, and applies to most of what you buy, including postage and professional services. However, books incur no provincial tax, and are often a bargain compared to elsewhere. Meals in restaurants are taxed, while most store-bought foods are not.

What to Buy?

Of course, what you're looking for depends on your personal preferences. Here are some broad categories.

Works of Art: Contemporary Quebec and Canadian paintings are available in galleries near the Museum of Fine Arts (on Sherbrooke and Crescent streets), and along Rue St-Paul Ouest in Old Montreal. The museum itself also has a gallery of art for sale, at 1390 Rue Sherbrooke Ouest. Inuit (Eskimo) carvings in soapstone and whalebone may be found at some of the galleries near the museum, at the *Canadian Guild of Crafts Québec* (2025 Rue Peel), as well as at shops in Old Montreal. *Le Chariot*, 446 Place Jacques-Cartier, is one source.

Crafts: Blown glass, leatherware, prints and smaller items are available at shops in Bonsecours Market and along Rue St-Paul and elsewhere in Old Montreal. Amerindian bead craft, jewelry, and leatherwork are widely available in souvenir shops in Old Montreal.

High Fashion: All of Montreal is high fashion! But if you have to look, consider *Holt Renfrew*, 1300 Sherbrooke Ouest, where the mandarins from Ottawa come to shop; *Ogilvy*, 1307 Rue Sainte-Catherine Ouest, a collection of independent high-fashion merchants; **Les Cours Mont-Royal**, Metcalfe at De Maisonneuve, a shopping complex connected to the Underground City, where a number of local 'name' designers have their boutiques; **Rue Sainte-Catherine** at Crescent and to the east, where labels such as *Parasuco* (corner of Crescent), *Mexx* (no 1125), *Guess* (no 1229), *Benetton* (no 1253) and Canadian icon *Roots* (no 1223) have stores; **Eaton Centre**, Rue Sainte-Catherine and McGill College Avenue, which includes shops such as *Benetton*; and *Simons*, 977 Sainte-Catherine Ouest, a new branch of the Quebec City fashion retailer.

A second and more avant-garde fashion area is **Rue St-Denis** north of Sherbrooke, around Rachel and Duluth, where Quebec name designers and those yet to make their names have shops; more familiar retailers such as *Gap* and *Mexx* have outposts as well. There are also fashionable boutiques in **Bonsecours Market** and along **Rue St-Paul** in Old Montreal.

Jewelry: The Tiffany's of Montreal, with fine smaller furnishings, is *Birk's*, on Phillips Square at Rue Sainte-Catherine. The fashion centers mentioned above also have jewelry items.

Food: Maple syrup, and items made from it, are available at food stores and gift shops. Much of the syrup sold in cans and bottles is graded Canada No 1 medium, though many prefer the richer taste of lower, darker grades of syrup (if you can find it). *Laura Secord* (Eaton Centre and other locations) is the quintessentially Canadian sweet shop (though owned by Nestlé). Smoked salmon in vacuum-sealed packaging, available at airport shops and some food stores, also travels well. Look in the gourmet foods section of *La Baie* department store for other items.

Inuit soapstone carvings.

Outdoor Wear: Montreal and Quebec are where much cold-weather gear is designed, if not always manufactured. Sorel boots, Kanuk parkas, Hors La Loi skiwear and more are available in many department stores. Or try such sportswear chains as *Sports Experts*, 930 Rue Sainte-Catherine Ouest, or more specialized shops such as *Kayakqua*, 1632 Rue Sherbrooke Ouest, or *L'Aventurier*, 1604 Rue St-Denis. *Kanuk* has a large store at 485 Rue Rachel Est, near Rue St-Denis.

Imports: If you can't get to Mexico, Guatemala, Tibet, or East Africa, you'll find household goods and clothing from these places and more in Latin Quarter boutiques along St-Denis, and, to a lesser degree, along St-Paul in Old Montreal.

Fur: The trade in furs built Montreal. You can choose between the manufacturers' showrooms, in the vicinity of Boulevard de Maisonneuve and Rue Aylmer; fur stores elsewhere, such as *Alexandor*, 2055 Rue Peel; and fur concessions at some of the department stores, such as *Holt Renfrew* and *Ogilvy*. Among fur showrooms are *McComber*, 402 Boulevard de Maisonneuve Ouest, *Bibergal*, 400 de Maisonneuve Ouest, and *Grossman and Grosvenor*, in the same building.

Antiques: Quebec pine furniture, as well as stained-glass windows, hardware rescued from demolition sites, and assorted collectibles, are offered in shops (or, more accurately, retail warehouses), along Rue Notre-Dame between Guy and Vinet (walk east from Atwater near metro Lionel-Groulx); and, to a lesser degree, along east-end Rue Amherst, above Sainte-Catherine. Reproduction furniture is on display in showrooms in Bonsecours Market and along Rue St-Paul.

Other Items: Cuban cigars – not to be brought to the United States – are a taste of the forbidden for Americans, available at any tobacconist. The same goes for Havana Club rum, stocked in liquor stores (SAQ, or Société des Alcools du Québec).

Shopping Meccas

If the weather is less than friendly, your priority shopping venues will probably be the indoor malls that connect with each other as the Underground City. Many of the shops have familiar names: Gap, Pier I (Import Bazaar), Levi's Outlet, Foot Locker, etc. Others will be strictly local mom-and-pop boutiques, or franchises operating under French names in Quebec. Canada has been a shopping paradise for even the most mundane of items over the last few years, so take your credit card and head for the malls.

In addition to **Eaton Centre** and **Les Cours Mont-Royal**, mentioned above, consider:

Place Montréal Trust, Rue Sainte-Catherine at McGill College Avenue.

Les Promenades de la Cathédrale, Rue Sainte-Catherine and University, under Christ Church Cathedral.

Place Ville-Marie, south end of McGill College Avenue, where the shops are placed along underground 'streets,' rather than around galleries.

All of the above have food courts and restaurants to fortify you for your excursion.

The last remaining large traditional department store downtown is **La Baie** (**The Bay**, or **Hudson's Bay Company**), 585 Rue Sainte-Catherine Ouest, with everything from sandals to major appliances, but concentrating on mid-range clothing.

The shopping malls above tend toward smaller outlets of brand-name stores and upscale boutiques. For a more suburban Canadian shopping experience, visit one of the larger indoor concourses that is easily accessible by metro.

Place Versailles, in the east end of the city at the Radisson metro station, has several hundred stores, ranging from *Radio Shack*, *Cohoes* discount fashion, *Centre HiFi* or *Au Coton* fashion, to a hardware store and a branch of *La Baie* department store, not to mention a cinema, and food outlets with poutine, Lebanese fare, and more. Across the street is an equally huge *Loblaws* food supermarket. Come out this way after visiting the Olympic Stadium and Botanical Gardens.

Service at Place Versailles is almost exclusively in French. If you're more comfortable in a mixed English-French environment, visit **Carrefour Angrignon**, two blocks north of the Angrignon metro station in suburban LaSalle, south-west of downtown.

The Eaton Centre.

ENTERTAINMENT AND NIGHTLIFE

The best of Montreal is free. Stroll from free concert to free concert in the open at the annual Festival International de Jazz or the Festival Nuits d'Afrique. Pause along Rue Jeanne-Mance to join the crowds around a stilt walker, a fire-eater, a unicyclist or a juggler (donation appreciated).

Mix with the crowds on Place Jacques-Cartier by the Old Port, and bump into a white-painted statue that turns out to be alive!

Watch the skating and tobogganing in Mount Royal Park in winter, from the warmth of a chalet … or see the citizenry parade past your perch at a sidewalk café on Rue Prince-Arthur or Rue St-Denis.

But there's even more on offer, of course, for a modest admission fee or cover charge. For current performances of Montreal-based and visiting companies, check listings in newspapers, especially the *Gazette* and *La Presse*. Free alternative newspapers with movie, music and restaurant listings, ads and coupons, include *The Mirror* and *Hour* in English, and *Voir* and *Ici* in French. They're available on racks at supermarket and trendy restaurant entrances, and near schools and universities.

Music Companies

The **Orchestre Symphonique de Montréal** (Montreal Symphony Orchestra), under Charles Dutoit, performs at Salle Wilfrid-Pelletier, Place des Arts (175 Rue Sainte-Catherine Ouest, ☎ 514 842 9951).

The smaller **Orchestre Métropolitain** usually performs at Théâtre Maisonneuve on Place des Arts (☎ 514 598 0870), as does **L'Opéra de Montréal** (☎ 514 985 2258).

The **McGill Chamber Orchestra** and others perform at Pollack Concert Hall (555 Rue Sherbrooke Ouest, ☎ 514 398 4547). **I Musici de Montréal** (934 Rue Sainte-Catherine Est, ☎ 514 982 6037) perform chamber works.

Jazz

Montreal has been a jazz city since prohibition days. Such greats as Oscar Peterson are strictly home-grown. A long-time hot spot is **L'Air du Temps**, 191 Rue St-Paul Ouest, in Old Montreal. Downtown is **Biddle's**, 2060 Rue Aylmer, which also serves complete meals (cover charge at both).

Rock

The really big acts play at the **Molson Centre** hockey palace. Normal-sized acts appear at the **Spectrum** (318 Rue Sainte-Catherine Ouest, ☎ 514 861 5851), with seating at tables (tickets generally $20 or less) and at **Le Medley** (1170 Rue St-Denis,

☎ 514 842 6557).

Café Campus, 57 Rue Prince-Arthur Est, has live rock music on many nights, with cheap pitchers of beer and a low cover charge.

Hard Rock Café (1458 Rue Crescent) serves a familiar formula of rock videos and American-style food.

Metropolis (59 Rue Sainte-Catherine Est) is a multi-bar, dance hall complex, with music that ranges from current rock to jazz.

Irish

Hurley's Irish Pub (1225 Rue Crescent) and **Vieux Dublin** (1219A Rue University) are more pub-like than many a locale in Ireland, and have live music many nights.

World

Club Balattou (4372 Boulevard St-Laurent) has dance music from Africa and the Americas, every night except Monday.

Comedy

Comedyworks (1238 Rue Bishop, ☎ 514 398 9661) is home to English-language improvisations and one-liners. Shows are at 9pm most nights.

Comedy Nest (1740 Boulevard René-Lévesque, ☎ 514 932 6378) has shows on Thursdays to Saturdays at $10 or less, with dinner-and-show packages.

French-language comedy is largely seen on television or at the annual Just for Laughs Festival. The **Cabaret Les Amuseurs** of the Musée Juste Pour Rire (Just for Laughs Museum, 2111 Boulevard St-Laurent, ☎ 514 845 4000) regularly has performances.

Occasionally, impressionists will appear at Théâtre St-Denis or other venues in the Latin Quarter.

Theater/Théâtre

The **Centaur**, (453 Rue St-François-Xavier, ☎ 514 288 3161), in a former stock exchange, is Montreal's main English-language theater. Works by Québecois authors are occasionally performed in translation.

Works in French are performed largely in theaters toward the eastern end of downtown: the **Monument National**, home of the National Theater School (1182 Boulevard St-Laurent, ☎ 514 842 7954); **Théâtre d'Aujourd'hui** (3900 Rue St-Denis, ☎ 514 282

Live jazz at Biddle's.

3900); **Théâtre du Nouveau Monde** (84 Rue Sainte-Catherine Ouest, ☎ **514 866 8668**); and **Théâtre St-Denis** (1594 Rue St-Denis, ☎ **514 849 4211**). **Théâtre de Quat'Sous** (100 Avenue Des Pins Est, ☎ **514 845 7277**) is an alternative French-language theater. **Theatre du Rideau Vert** (4664 St-Denis ☎ **514 844 1793**) is one of the oldest theaters.

Montreal is one of the few places where **Yiddish-language** plays are presented regularly, at the **Saidye Bronfman Center** (5170 Chemin Côte-Sainte-Catherine, ☎ **514 739 7944**).

Dance

Major Montreal-based companies include **Les Grands Ballets Canadiens** (☎ **514 849 0269**) and **Les Ballets Jazz de Montréal** (☎ **514 982 6771**).

Movies

Don't go by the title of a movie alone. Any film might show in French with English subtitles, in English with French subtitles, in French only (most likely), English only, or in another language. The fine print in ads includes '*v. o. anglaise*' (original English version), '*v. o. française*' (French version), '*s. t. français*' (French subtitles), etc. (French abbreviations often appear in English-language media.) Individual film prices rarely top $9, and are lower at most cinemas in the afternoon,

and on Tuesdays and Wednesdays.

One of the more interesting locales for viewing films is the **Ex-Centris** nouveau cinema complex (3536 Boulevard St-Laurent, ☎ **514 847 3536**). Classics and avant garde films may also be viewed at the **National Film Board** (Office National du Film, 1564 Rue St-Denis, ☎ **514 496 6887**) and the **Cinémathèque Québecoise** (335 Boulevard de Maisonneuve Est, ☎ **514 842 9763**). Offbeat films can be viewed at **Cinéma Parallèle**, a compact room behind the café at 3536 Boulevard St-Laurent.

The **IMAX** cinema, in the Old Port (☎ **514 496 4629**) has a seasonal offering of spectacular large-screen films at admission prices of $12.50 or less. The annual **World Film Festival** takes place late August to early September.

Bars

Sir Winston Churchill Pub (1459 Rue Crescent) is a long-standing and friendly basement bar. Upstairs is a more formal eatery and dance hall.

Peel Pub (1107 Rue Sainte-Catherine Ouest) plays recorded rock music and serves inexpensive food, including bargain breakfasts.

Cheers (1260 Rue Mackay) is as friendly as the TV bar for which it's named, and serves a lunch buffet.

Thursdays, or **Les Beaux Jeudis** (1449 Rue Crescent), long-standing see-and-be-seen place, plays recorded music and has a more formal restaurant with accomplished salads.

In the Gay Village, **Aigle Noir** (1315 Rue Sainte-Catherine Est), is only closed for a few hours of the day. **Sisters** (1333 Rue Sainte-Catherine Est) is a gay and lesbian bar.

History
For a trip back to Nouvelle France, **Le Festin du Gouverneur** (on St Helen's Island) serves a fixed-course banquet with music and comedy, at about $40 (every night May-Oct, weekends the rest of the year; ☎ 514 879 1141).

Gambling
Montreal's **Casino** offers magnificent views, along with blackjack, slot machines, keno, poker, roulette and midi-baccarat. One of the big attractions is that no tax cut is taken on winnings. Neat dress is required for admittance. Minimum age is 18.

Amusement Park
La Ronde, at the downriver end of St Helen's Island, is Montreal's large summer amusement park. Vertigo-inducing rides in ever-evolving manifestations are the bill of fare, though there are tamer bumper cars and log-flume rides for non-thrill seekers, as well as on-site entertainment and eateries. The admission price is lower than at similar parks elsewhere (family discounts available), and includes unlimited access to rides (for information ☎ 514 872 6222).

SPORTS

Spectator Sports
The legendary Montreal Canadiens, winners of more Stanley Cups than any other **hockey** team, play at the Molson Centre (Rue Stanley at De La Gauchetière, *metro:* Lucien L'Allier). The season runs from late fall to mid-spring. Tickets cost from $18 to $125, and many games are sold out (for information ☎ 514 932 2582).

Baseball is played from April until October, under the roof of the Olympic Stadium in the east end (*metro:* Pie-IX). Tickets to Expos games run from $8 to $36, and can usually be purchased on-site (☎ 514 846 3976).

Canadian Football is considered more exciting than the American variety, with more passing and kicking and a wide-open style of play on a larger field. The Alouettes play at the intimate Molson Stadium on the campus of McGill University, just north of downtown. The season runs from late July to November. Tickets cost from $13 to $45 (for information ☎ 514 871 2255).

Automobile Racing

The annual Formula 1 **Grand Prix du Canada** takes place on Notre Dame Island every June.

Participatory Sports

Skating

Outdoor rinks are opened every winter in many city parks. There's also skating in winter at Beaver Lake (Lac aux Castors) in Mount Royal Park, and at the Old Port and on St Helen's Island.

The rink at the **Atrium**, 1000 Rue de la Gauchetière (☎ **514 395 0555**), near Central Station, is open all year, for a fee of $5 or less. Rental skates are available.

Golf

Golf courses that allow play by visitors include **Le Village** (Olympic Park, ☎ **514 872 4653**), **Dorval Golf Club** (☎ **514 631 4653**), **Dorval Municipal Golf Course** (☎ **514 631 4711**), and **Meadowbrook Golf Club** (☎ **514 488 6612**).

Skiing

Some of the best **cross-country ski** trails, ranging from level to up-and-down, are just above downtown in Mount Royal Park. Access is from the transverse road, reached either by car or bus no 11 from metro Mont-Royal, or by walking up Rue Peel. Other trails are in Maisonneuve Park, near the Olympic Stadium, and in several suburban parks in the north-western part of the island, including Bois de Liesse and Cap St-Jacques.

Cross-country skis are rented by **La Poubelle de Ski** (8278 Boulevard St-Laurent, ☎ **514 384 1315**) and **The Ski Exchange** (54 Avenue Westminster North, Montreal West, ☎ **514 486 2849**).

The nearest **downhill ski** resorts are at Mont St-Sauveur (☎ **514 871 0101**), 60km (37 miles) north of Montreal, and Bromont (☎ **888 866 4270**), about 70km (44 miles) to the east. And there are many others, topping out at Mont Tremblant (☎ **800 567 6760**), 120km (75 miles) to the north, with the most comprehensive facilities (*see* p.87). Discount tickets to some ski areas are available at Costco warehouse stores (membership is required) and in conjunction with car rentals.

Cycling

Montreal is bicycle-friendly. Cycling routes run to the west, north, and east from downtown. Most are reserved strips along the vehicular right of way, but a few are linear parks where vehicles can't intrude, even accidentally.

The park-like Lachine Canal path runs from the Old Port westward along the Lachine Canal through one of the first industrial areas on the continent (which is now giving way to gentrification). A branch route runs south-westward from Lachine back along the St Lawrence, past the Lachine Rapids to downtown, allowing a circular trip.

Another branch from the Lachine Canal route, just beyond Old Montreal, runs to and through Parc Jean Drapeau – Notre Dame and St Helen's islands. On a fair day, a bicycle is the best way to see Montreal's islands.

Bicycles are available for rent at **Vélo-Tour** (99 Rue de la Commune Ouest, ☎ 514 236 8356); from an outlet in Info-touriste, the downtown tourist office (☎ 514 878 3847); and from **La Cordée Vélo** (2159 Rue Papineau Est, ☎ 514 524 1515). Fees can be as high as $20 daily, with helmet, and for usage over several days it's almost as cheap to buy a used bike. One source is **Lazy Walker** (5526 Rue Sherbrooke Ouest, ☎ 514 481 5159, *metro:* Vendôme, bus no 105). For guided bicycle tours, *see* p.125.

Swimming

Outdoor pools are available in many city parks, for a fee. Easily accessible is one on St Helen's Island (*metro:* Île Ste-Hélène). A beach and lagoon are not far away on Notre Dame Island.

The most spectacular indoor pool is the huge Piscine Olympique (*metro:* Viau), adjacent to the Olympic Stadium, open to general swimming when competitions are not in progress (☎ 514 252 4622 for hours).

Birdwatching

For birdwatchers, the hot spot is Summit Park in Westmount, a haven of wild land atop slopes dotted with mansions (bus nos 165 or 166 from metro Guy-Concordia, walk up Belvedere Road, or take a taxi.) Sightings in the much larger Mount Royal Park, with its wide open spaces, are more elusive.

Kayaking and Rowing

Rowboats are available for rent in summer at the artificial lake on **Notre Dame Island** (*metro:* Île Ste-Hélène, bus no 167). For a longer run through idyllic waters, rent a rowboat, kayak or canoe at **Parc des Îles de Boucherville** near the south end of the Lafontaine Tunnel, opposite Montreal, most easily accessible by car or ferry in summer (☎ 514 281 8000 for details).

Cross-country skiers near Val David.

THE BASICS

Before You Go

British visitors to Canada will need a current passport. US citizens need only proof of citizenship, and permanent residents of the US need proof of their citizenship and status in the US, such as a 'green card'.

No visas are required of citizens of Western European countries, including Hungary, though immigration officials have the right to restrict length of stay, depending on circumstances. Citizens of Australia, New Zealand, Israel, Costa Rica and the Bahamas, among other nations, may also enter without a visa, as may British citizens and overseas British passport holders who have the right of re-admission to the UK.

Citizens of countries not mentioned above should consult a Canadian consulate about current visa requirements. These are summarized on the web at www.cic.gc.ca/English/visit.

Vaccinations are generally not required, except for persons arriving from countries where there have been recent outbreaks of communicable diseases.

Getting There

By Air

Most international flights arrive at **Dorval Airport** (☎ **514 633**

3105), situated 22km (14 miles) west of downtown Montreal. **L'Aérobus** (☎ **514 931 9002**) operates a direct airport bus service from 5am to midnight from 777 Rue de la Gauchetière Ouest, next to Central Station (fare $11, $20 round-trip). A shuttle service is provided to major downtown hotels. From the airport, the direct bus service operates from 7am to 1am. A taxi to downtown costs $25 to $30 and takes around half an hour, depending on traffic.

To reach the airport by public transportation, but only with limited luggage, take bus no 211 from metro Lionel-Groulx one stop to the Dorval commuter terminal, and transfer to the westbound no 204 bus which passes the airport terminal.

Mirabel Airport, 55km (34 miles) north-west of the city, serves cargo and charter flights. For information and departure times ☎ **514 931 9002** or www.admtl.com. L'Aérobus services operate hourly, starting at 1.55am most days from downtown, 3am from the airport. The fare is $18, $25 round-trip. A taxi from Mirabel to downtown costs about $65 and takes around 45 minutes.

By Rail

Via Rail, Canada's national railway company, offers swift downtown-to-downtown service along the heavily populated 'Corridor' stretching from Windsor (near Detroit), through Toronto to Montreal and Quebec City. Connections are available from across Canada, and from all points on the US **Amtrak** system. A recent useful addition is an overnight sleeping-car service to and from Toronto, saving the cost of a hotel room. Via 1 first-class service includes meals and beverages.

Via Rail **tickets** are sold by many travel agents, by phone (☎ 514 989 2626 or 800 361 5390), or at www.viarail.ca. Discounts are available to students, seniors and children, and with advance purchase. For Amtrak tickets, call ☎ 800 872 7245.

By Bus
Montreal is connected by bus to all cities in Quebec, Canada and the United States. Bus travel is the most inexpensive way to travel if tickets are purchased well in advance, or with a discount arrangement, such as Greyhound's Ameripass.

Montreal's central bus station, **Terminus Voyageur**, is at the corner of De Maisonneuve and Berri, on the eastern edge of downtown. For information on all bus services from Montreal, call ☎ 514 842 2281. For Greyhound, call ☎ 800 231 2222 in the US, ☎ 800 661 8747 in Canada, or see www.greyhound.com.

By Car
Montreal is within a day's drive of Washington DC, New York, Boston and Toronto via major expressways and connecting autoroutes.

White-knuckle ride at La Ronde amusement park.

A-Z

Accidents and Breakdowns

Police should be called following any accident, ☎ 911. When possible, a Joint Report of Automobile Accident (which local drivers carry) should be filled out.

Car rental companies will provide a number to call in case of accident or mechanical problems. Your automobile club, roadside assistance plan, or vehicle warranty service may be able to provide a toll-free number to call in case of breakdown.

Accommodations see p. 93

Airports see Getting There, p. 112

Alcoholic Beverages

The legal age for consumption of alcohol is 18. Spirits and most wines are sold at outlets of the provincially owned Société des Alcools du Québec. A limited assortment of cheaper wines is available in convenience stores (*dépanneurs*) and supermarkets. Some restaurants invite you to bring your own wine (*apportez votre vin*).

Banks, Currency and Exchange

The $ symbol in this book indicates Canadian dollars. Canadian currency is issued in banknotes in denominations of 5, 10, 20, 50, 100, 500 and 1 000, and in coins of $2 ('two-nie'), $1 ('loonie,' or '*pièce*'), 25 cents ('quarter'), 10 cents ('dime'), 5 cents ('nickel') and 1 cent ('penny' or '*sou*').

Banks' opening hours are generally Mon-Fri 9.30am-3pm, with local variations (with Thursday evening and Saturday opening).

Banks will exchange US and Canadian dollars, sterling, and sometimes euro travelers' checks (cheques), usually at graduated rates depending on the amount. Better rates for travelers' checks, and for major foreign currencies, are usually available at the exchange bureaus located in the vicinity of Peel and Sainte-Catherine streets, downtown. Many stores accept US dollars, but at disadvantageous rates.

The best exchange rates are generally offered on purchases made directly by credit card (Visa and Master Card are the most widely accepted, even at supermarkets); and on automated teller machines (cash point) withdrawals. Rates, commissions and service fees vary from bank to bank.

Bicycles see Cycling, p. 110

Breakdowns see Accidents

Buses see Transport

Car Rental

A car is not really needed for getting around Montreal; indeed, you might enjoy your visit more if you don't have to worry about parking. But for visits to suburban sites and nearby parks and ski areas, a rental vehicle will come in handy.

Rates vary by season and according to how you book. The best rates are generally found through Internet travel sites. The highest rates are for on-the-spot rentals. Most companies have toll-free reservations numbers.

Choose your rate plan – unlimited kilometers or fee per kilometer – according to your itinerary. Extra charges are incurred for a second driver, and for a driver under the age of 25. A credit card is required to avoid leaving a large cash deposit. Gold and platinum credit cards generally provide insurance cover that will substitute for expensive cover through the car-rental company.

A selection of main car rental agencies:

Avis ☎ 800 321 3652
Budget ☎ 800 268 8900
Hertz ☎ 800 263 0678
Thrifty ☎ 800 367 2277

Children

The practice in most Canadian hotels is not to charge for children under 18 sharing a room with parents. Child-minding services are available in larger hotels.

There are reduced admission prices for children at museums, skating rinks, cinemas and many other venues.

Festivals in Montreal are great for children as well as for adults. There are always street entertainers at the Jazz Fest and other summer events.

Street animators, buskers, clowns, living statues and balloon artists liven up **Place Jacques-Cartier** and nearby streets, in Old Montreal.

Attractions in the **Old Port** include the **IMAX** supersize cinema, and yet more roving entertainers, a motorized tram, music and seasonal shows.

Youngsters and older children will enjoy the 50-minute multimedia astronomy shows, in both English and French, at **Le Planétarium de Montréal** (Dow Planetarium), south of downtown (1000 St-Jacques West, *metro:* Bonaventure ☎ 872 4530 for details).

Aside from pools, parks and playgrounds, the **Atrium** skating rink (*see* p. 110) is open all year. **Laser Quest** (1226 Rue Sainte-Catherine Ouest, ☎ 514 393 3000) will keep youngsters amused for several hours.

The **Ecomuseum** in Ste-Anne-de-Bellevue (see p. 86) houses live animals from the St Lawrence Valley, while **Cap St-Jacques Regional Park** near the north-west edge of the island has a small working farm.

Libraries throughout the city host story hours in English and French. One with Wednesday readings is the Westmount Library (4574 Rue Sherbrooke Ouest, ☎ 514 989 5300).

Climate see p. 91

Clothing

Casual clothing is appropriate for sightseeing in Montreal. Jeans, shorts and sandals are acceptable in warm weather for most activities and in most mid priced restaurants. A tie and jacket, or dress, should be worn in formal restaurants, at the theater and at concerts.

Of course, you'll take what's appropriate for the season, including an overcoat, boots, hat, gloves and scarf or neck warmer in winter, and an umbrella for spring, summer and

Young and old take to their wheels in Montreal.

fall. A hat is useful as sun protection during the long northern summer days.

What to do with winter footwear is a social quandary for those unfamiliar with the climate. Montrealers most often have formal winter boots, which they can wipe off and wear comfortably inside restaurants. Or they'll carry a pair of slip-on shoes, and on arrival leave their heavy boots along with their coats. You can follow the latter procedure when visiting a private home, or simply remove your boots and enter in your stockinged feet.

Clothing is generally low-priced and a wise purchase. Sizes are as in the US. Shoes are often labelled in US, UK and European systems.

Womcn's sizes

UK	8	10	12	14	16	18
Italy	38	40	42	44	46	48
US	6	8	10	12	14	16

Women's shoes

UK	4.5	5	5.5	6	6.5	7
Italy	38	38	39	39	40	41
US	6	6.5	7	7.5	8	8.5

Men's suits

UK/US	36	38	40	42	44	46
Italy	46	48	50	52	54	56

Men's shirts

UK/US	14	14.5	15	15.5	16	16.5	17
Italy	36	37	38	39/40	41	42	43

Men's shoes

UK	7	7.5	8.5	9.5	10.5	11
Italy	41	42	43	44	45	46
US	8	8.5	9.5	10.5	11.5	12

Consulates
UK
1000 Rue de la Gauchetière Ouest, Montreal H3B 4W5
☎ **514 866 5863**
USA
1155 Rue St-Alexandre, Place Félix-Martin, Montreal H2Z 1Z2
☎ **514 398 9695**

Crime
Criminal activities in Montreal, such as they are, tend toward bank robbery and auto theft, rather than crime against individuals. Montrealers generally feel safe on the streets at all hours. Of course, visitors, unfamiliar with the local scene, can be more easily victimized than locals. Follow the usual precautions:

• Leave excess cash, jewelry and credit cards in the safe at your hotel.

• Use inside or hidden pockets for valuables, and hold your handbag firmly.

• Lock your car (rented or your own), with valuables out of view, or removed.

• Be cautious of strangers in crowds.

• Report theft to the police ☎ **911** and loss of a passport to your consulate.

Disabled Visitors
Most hotels and tourist attractions have wheelchair access, but to a limited degree only. You can

obtain the guide *Accès-tourisme* ($15 plus $5 postage) from KEROUL, 4545 Pierre-de-Coubertin Ave, CP 1000 Montreal (Qc) H1V 3RZ. The *Handy Travel* guide ($12.95 plus postage) is available from the Canadian Rehabilitation Council for the Disabled, 90 Eglinton Ave Est, Suite 511, Toronto (ON) M4P 2Y3. Information about specific facilities is available at ☎ 514 252 3104, by e-mail at croy@keroul.qc.ca, or on the web at www.keroul.qc.ca.

Public transportation for disabled persons is available to residents by direct arrangement. Bus lines 11, 14, 27, 51 and 97 in the central area are handicapped-accessible outside of rush hours. For additional lines, check the public transportation web site www.stcum.qc.ca.

Driving

While downtown traffic is not appalling, compared to other cities, expressways are often bottlenecked. Since attractions are concentrated in a small area, consider leaving your car at home, or garaging it once you arrive. Local challenges include snowy streets in winter, until cleared; a scarcity of on-street parking; and the propensity of Montrealers to jaywalk in disregard of their own safety.

US and international driving licenses are valid in Quebec, and US insurance policies will provide coverage. The minimum driving age is 18.

Directional and safety signs are in French, usually with enough pictograms or familiar symbols to make them comprehensible to English-speakers. If you don't understand a sign, ask a passerby.

Driving is on the right, and seat belts must be worn. There is some tolerance of driving over the speed limit (30-50km per hour on Montreal streets). Illegally parked cars are subject to towing.

Gasoline (petrol) generally costs about one-third more in Quebec than in adjacent American states, but is much cheaper than in Europe.

Electric Current

Electricity is supplied at 110 volts AC, 60Hz, as in the USA. Sockets accept a plug with two parallel flat prongs and grounding pin, so an adaptor is needed for UK appliances. Many hotel bathrooms have an outlet that supplies current at 220 volts and which will accept a two-pin plug. Appliances with motors may not work properly without transformers.

Embassies *see* Consulates

Emergencies

Dial **911** for assistance with all

police, fire or health emergencies. Operators can handle calls in English and French.

Guidebooks see Maps

Health
Visitors from elsewhere in Canada should carry their own provincial medical insurance card, but should verify coverage before leaving home.

Visitors from outside Canada should check that their national health plan or private insurance provides cover in Canada, and arrange alternative insurance before departure if not.

Waiting times in hospital emergency rooms can be long. Non-urgent matters can be dealt with at walk-in medical clinics, listed in the telephone directory under 'Clinics – Medical'. One centrally located clinic is **Metro Medic**, 1253 Rue Guy (☎ 514 932 2122). Public health centers (called CLSCs) will attend to visitors but at higher rates than private clinics. For dental emergencies call the 24-hour line ☎ 514 342 4444.

Most doctors in central and western Montreal can deal with patients in English. Only selected hospitals are authorized to provide services in English (notably the Montreal General Hospital and Royal Victoria Hospital near downtown).

Hours see Opening Hours

Competitors in the Tour d l'Île cycle marathon.

Information see **Tourist Information**

Internet

If you have a portable computer, it's best to verify local access numbers for your ISP before leaving home. Do not connect to a hotel phone system before checking compatibility of the phone lines.

Public web access is available at airport terminals and hotel business centers, but at the highest rates (as much as $30 per hour). For lower rates at a convenient location, check the French Yellow Pages under *Internet-Cafés*, or try the *Chapters* bookstore, at the corner of Rue Sainte-Catherine and Stanley.

Language

French, of course, is the language of living, loving, business and just about everything else in Montreal. The allure of the city for many, despite its many other attractions, is that Montreal is so accessible, in its layout and services, yet so exotic at the same time because of its French heritage.

Local people will understand French as spoken by visitors from elsewhere. The reverse isn't always true. Within Montreal, there are differences in the language spoken by different social classes, and in local vocabulary and expressions. A *biscuit salé* (cracker) is a *craquelin* in Quebec, *les parfums de la crème glacée* (flavors of ice cream) are *saveurs*. Shopping is *le magasinage*.

None of this local usage is insurmountable, however, and those who have a knowledge of French will easily understand the language as spoken in stores, on news broadcasts, and in restaurants and hotels.

And for those who don't speak French, just a few words will go far in expressing your appreciation that French is the *lingua franca*. *Bonjour!* (hello), *bonsoir* (good evening) *oui* (yes) and even *non* (no) with a pleasant expression will take you far.

Despite Montreal's French heart and face – almost all commercial signs are in the local tongue – English is widely but not *inevitably* understood. English is spoken and used in business downtown, and in the west end of the city and the western suburbs. Most telephone information lines offer an option of messages in English or French. Hotel personnel generally speak English, but not so all restaurant waiters. The driver of a city bus might have a rudimentary knowledge of English, or just might be an *anglophone* working in a French environment, as most Montrealers do. In general, a visitor can expect a welcome and assistance in his or her own language, but as a matter of politeness, should never demand it.

Other languages that the visitor will encounter in the central area, spoken by immigrant or second-generation Montrealers, include Spanish, Arabic, Cantonese, Greek and

Italian. Spanish is understood to some extent by many French-speakers, who feel an affinity toward Latin neighbors to the south.

Maps and Guidebooks

The *Michelin Green Guide Quebec* provides detailed maps of Montreal and the various neighborhoods, plus full information on the main attractions and other sights. It also includes details of the excursions you may wish to make from Montreal. Free maps, brochures, and metro and bus maps are provided by the tourist information centres (*see* **Tourist Information**). Car rental agencies also provide free maps to help with general route planning and driving.

A large-scale motoring map, which may be purchased from any bookstore, is ideal for touring outside Montreal.

Medical Care *see* Health

Money *see* Banks, Currency and Exchange

Newspapers

Montreal's English-language newspaper is *The Gazette*. In addition, the *Globe and Mail* and the *National Post*, based in Toronto, circulate locally. Major US papers are widely available.

French-language dailies

English / Canadian French
yes / oui
no / non
please / s'il vous plaît
thank you / merci
you're welcome / bienvenue
hello, good morning / bonjour
goodbye / bye
how much / combien?
where? / où?
I don't understand / je ne comprends pas
do you speak English / parlez-vous anglais?
breakfast / déjeuner
lunch / dîner
dinner / souper
expressway, motorway / autoroute
gasoline, petrol / essence
collect call / appel à frais virés
subway, underground / métro

include *La Presse*, with the most extensive coverage of news, the highbrow *Le Devoir*, and the tabloid *Journal de Montréal*.

Opening Hours

Shops: General **store** hours are 9am-6pm during the week, to 5pm on Saturdays. **Department stores** and many stores in shopping malls stay open until 9pm on Thursday and Friday, and open noon-5pm on Sunday. Smaller **supermarkets** observe general business hours, or close on Sunday; larger ones open 8am-11pm six days a week, and sometimes until 5pm or later on Sunday.

Chemists: Large pharmacies, such as *Pharmaprix* and *Jean Coutu*, which also sell general merchandise and food items, open at least 9am-9pm seven days a week. Convenience food stores (*dépanneurs*) observe similar long hours.

Tourist attractions such as museums generally open 10am-5pm, with much variation according to season, and many close on Monday.

Office business hours are generally 8.30/9am-5/5.30pm. *See also* **Postal Services** and **Banks, Currency and Exchange**

Photography

Film is easy to purchase at pharmacies, department stores, supermarkets, *dépanneurs* and photography stores in shopping malls. Photo processing is found in the same locations.

Police

Dial ☎ **911** for assistance from the metropolitan police (Service de la police de la communauté urbaine de Montréal). Officers assigned to the downtown area generally can speak enough English to communicate with visitors. Highways are patrolled by officers of the Sûreté du Québec, the provincial police department. The Royal Canadian Mounted Police (Gendarmerie du Canada) have limited functions in the province.

Postal Services

Post offices are open 8am-5pm, and most are closed on Saturday. Use them mainly for mailing packages. It is more convenient to buy stamps at convenience stores (*dépanneurs*) and tobacconists, at no extra cost, and at postal counters in pharmacies. The main downtown post offices are at 1250 Rue University and 1974 Rue Sainte-Catherine Ouest.

Postage is subject to sales tax. A stamp for Canada currently costs 46 cents; for the US, 55 cents; for other countries, 95 cents.

For general postal information, call ☎ **800 267 1177**.

Public Holidays

Businesses generally close on the holidays mentioned below, though degree of observance varies with the holiday. Petrol stations close on Easter Sunday and Christmas.

New Year's Day 1 January
Good Friday
Easter Sunday
Dollard Day (Victoria Day)
    3rd Monday in May
St Jean Baptiste 24 June
Canada Day 1 July
Labor Day First Monday in
    September
Thanksgiving Second Monday in
    October
Christmas 25 December
Boxing Day 26 December
    Remembrance Day, 11 November, is widely observed, with banks and government offices closed, but is not officially a public holiday.

Religion

All major religions are represented in Montreal. For places of worship, consult the yellow pages under 'Churches,' 'Mosques,' 'Synagogues,' etc.

Sightseeing see Tours

Smoking

Cigarette-smoking is more widespread in Quebec than elsewhere in North America, but is controlled in public places. Smoking is prohibited in office buildings and stores, and on buses and trains. A ban on smoking in restaurants is not widely enforced, but a non-smoking table can be requested.

Prices of tobacco products are lower than in many countries of Europe, but users might nevertheless want to stock up on duty-free supplies.

Taxis see Transport

Telephones

Pay phones are operated with coins (25 cents for local calls), or with magnetic cards purchased from vending machines or pharmacies. Different cards are used for local and long-distance calls. Credit cards may also be inserted – verify the charge on the display before completing the call; charges vary with different cards. There are no time charges on local calls. No coin is needed for toll-free (freephone) calls to numbers starting with **800**, **888**, or **877**.

The area code for Montreal island is **514**; for surrounding areas, **450**. Dial numbers in the adjacent area code without the **1** prefix. If it's considered long-distance, you'll hear a recorded message, and will have to redial with the prefix **1**, and pay by the minute.

A bewildering array of options is available for calling to foreign countries: collect from any phone; by paying in coins or with a phone card or credit card from a pay phone; by home-country direct numbers; by discount calling cards purchased at tobacconists and convenience stores (usually the cheapest way; instructions are on the cards); and by calling through the hotel operator (the most expensive).

Direct-dialled long-distance calls from Montreal to Canada, the US or the Caribbean are preceded by **1**; to other countries, by **011**. Use the prefixes **0** and **01**, respectively, for collect calls, and from pay phones. Country codes include: Australia **61**, Belgium **32**, France **33**, Ireland **353**, Luxembourg **352**, New Zealand **64**, Switzerland **41**, UK **44**.

Toll-free **Home Direct** numbers connect with operators in foreign countries. These include:
Australia ☎ **800 663 0683**
New Zealand ☎ **800 663 0684**
UK ☎ **800 363 4144**

Dial **0** to request other Home Direct numbers from the operator.

Call **411** for local directory enquiries (at a charge), **1** plus area code plus **555 1212** for numbers in other regions of the United States and Canada.

Time

Montreal is in the Eastern time zone of North America, along with New York and Miami, equivalent to Greenwich Mean Time less five hours. Clocks are advanced one hour for daylight saving time from April to October.

Tipping

Restaurant prices do not include tax and service. Tax of approximately 15 per cent is added, and tipping is at the discretion of the client, usually from 10 to 15 per cent. A similar range of tip applies to taxi fares. Porters at hotels may be given a dollar or so for one or two light bags. Tour guides and cloakroom attendants may expect a small tip, but it is not the practice to tip service station attendants or cinema personnel.

Tourist Information

The main tourist office in Montreal is **Centre Infotouriste** on Dorchester Square. Open 1 June-Labor Day daily 8.30am-7.30pm, Labor Day-31 May daily 9am-6pm. You can arrange tours, make hotel bookings, hire cars, obtain maps and information brochures, and the helpful bilingual staff will be able to assist with your enquiries. A second smaller office is at 174 Rue Notre-Dame Est, in Old Montreal.

For tourism information in Montreal, ☎ **514 873 2015**. From anywhere else in Canada or the

United States, ☎ 800 363 7777 or 877 BONJOUR (877 266 5687).

On the Web, see www.tourism-montreal.org. The **Tourisme Québec** site is www.bonjourquebec.com.

To obtain information before you leave home, contact:

UK
Délégation du Québec, 59 Pall Mall, London, SW1Y 5JH
☎ 020 7930 8314
or
Bridge Marketing, P O Box 1939, Maidenhead, Berkshire, SL6 1AJ
☎ 0990 561 705

USA
Délégation du Québec,
1 Rockefeller Plaza, 26th Floor,
New York, NY 10020
☎ 2212 397 0200

Tours

Among many available excursions are:

Vélo-Tour Montréal (99 De la Commune Ouest, ☎ 514 236 8356). Bicycle tours in several languages.

Le Bâteau-Mouche (Old Port, ☎ 514 849 9952). Paris-style glassed-topped boat cruises, with dinner.

Montreal Guide Service (☎ 514 342 8994). Customized guide service in several languages.

Gray Line (Infotouriste, 1001 Dorchester Square, ☎ 514 934 1222) and **Tour de Ville** (Infotouriste, 1001 Dorchester Square, ☎ 514 871 4733).

General tours, in air-conditioned buses departing from Dorchester Square.

Guidatour (☎ 514 844 4021, 800 363 4021). Old Montreal walking tours.

Les Descentes sur le St-Laurent (Infotouriste, 1001 Dorchester Square, ☎ 514 767 2230, 800 324 7237) and **Saute-Moutons Jet Boating** (Old Port, ☎ 514 284 9607). Rafting and jet boating (involves a soaking) through the Lachine Rapids – take a sweater and a change of clothes!

Transport

Montreal is a walking city in spring, summer and autumn: compact, with few challenging slopes and hills. More than in most cities, the downtown streets

The World Trade Center.

are always alive with strollers. Pedestrians even assume they own the right of way, and jaywalk without a care, though visitors should not emulate the habit!

Winter is more challenging. The network of underground passages and arcades provides sheltered shortcuts, but at some point you'll have to face cold temperatures and streets which might not yet be completely cleared of snow. Dress accordingly.

Montreal's **metro** (underground) has a dense network of stations in the central area. Major lines reach northward and to the east and west, and even to Longueuil on the south shore of the St Lawrence River.

Buses are run by the same company as the metro, and cover much of the area served by the metro, as well as outlying districts. Service is more frequent in central areas. Maps of the public transit network, showing all streets, are available at metro ticket booths.

The fares for a single metro ride for any distance are bargains, at $2 Canadian (including free transfer to connecting bus routes), and $1.40 each in booklets of six tickets, available at metro ticket booths and convenience stores (*dépanneurs*). One-day ($7) and three-day ($14) tourist passes are available April-October at downtown metro stations, and all year round at the Berri-UQAM station. A better deal for visitors is a weekly pass, priced at only about $12.50, available during the first couple of days of the week at metro booths.

Lastly, **taxis** are relatively inexpensive, compared to those in other cities, at $2.25 to start, and $1.20 per km. Taxis may be flagged down, or called by phone. See listings in the Yellow Pages under *Taxis*.

TV and Radio

Most hotel and home televisions are connected to cable or satellite systems, offering programming in English, French, Spanish, and sometimes in other languages from Canada, the US, France, Latin America and elsewhere.

Local radio stations offer a variety of programming in English and French, and many nearby US stations can be picked up.

INDEX